*sixth edition*

# STUDY GUIDE

# CRIMINOLOGY
## Explaining Crime and Its Context

*Guide prepared by Maryann Stone*

*Stephen E. Brown*
Eastern Tennessee State University

*Finn-Aage Esbensen*
University of Missouri, St. Louis

*Gilbert Geis*
University of California, Irvine

LexisNexis®          **anderson publishing**
                     A member of the LexisNexis Group

## Criminology: Explaining Crime and Its Context, Sixth Edition
## STUDY GUIDE

Cover design by Tin Box Studio, Inc./Cincinnati, Ohio

EDITOR Janice Eccleston
ACQUISITIONS EDITOR Michael C. Braswell

# Preface

This study guide was prepared to supplement *Criminology: Explaining Crime and Its Context*, Sixth Edition. Each chapter follows a standard format by offering a summary of the chapter's content, definitions of essential key terms, and brief descriptions of the pertinent contributions of key criminologists. It is our hope that this study guide closely reflects the needs of beginning criminology students.

Criminology is an exciting field to study, but students are also concerned with examination performance. This study guide has been designed to assist you in your preparation for exams. Careful reading of your text, combined with thorough review of this study guide, should help you to understand the fundamental ideologies used to explain crime. We hope that this is one of the best classes in your college experience and that you have a more precise and critical perception of crime as a result.

Stephen E. Brown

# Table of Contents

# Chapter 1
# Crime and Criminology

## Summary

Although most people have opinions about crime, criminologists are professionally trained to study crime as an occupation. At the center of criminology is the study of crime. Crime, however, can be defined in many ways, even by criminologists.

Though criticized by some criminologists, studies using crime seriousness scales determine the public's opinion regarding which crimes are more serious than others. Such studies reveal a remarkable amount of consensus (agreement) among various members of the public, with violent crime ranked as more serious than property crimes. Yet, the public is often misinformed about crime.

## Criminology: Some Fundamentals

Criminology, according to most criminologists, is a science. The theoretical component of a science involves attempts to explain matters such as crime and criminalization (making an act illegal). The techniques or methods that criminologists use to try to prove or disprove theories rely on observation or data collection. However, some criminologists reject the scientific view of criminology, preferring to study how crime came to be defined rather than why it exists.

How criminologists define criminology is affected by their ideology, a set of beliefs or values of the way the world is or ought to be. Ideology cannot be removed from criminology, but we should be aware of its existence and the possible biases it can cause. Political ideological values fall along a continuum, ranging from politically liberal, or left-wing, to politically conservative, or right-wing. Typical of the left are concerns about liberty, over-criminalization, labeling, and discrimination by the criminal justice system, for they advocate enhancing social supports for those most at risk of offending. Typical of the right are concerns for the value of order, victim's rights, and calls for more punitive sanctions, as they tend to assume the offender is flawed or morally defective.

1

Ideology has caused problems such as gender subordination in criminology. Differing ideologies also cause criminologists to view the purpose of their work differently. As a science, criminology often is assumed to be value-free, but separating values from intellectual inquiry is not an easy task. Gender subordination, under which issues pertinent to females have been neglected and misrepresented, is just one consequence of ideology. Moreover, the changing definition of crime, or relativity of law, is largely driven by ideology.

## The "Crime" in Criminology

Criminologists define crime along a continuum. At one end of the continuum is a legalistic definition, describing crime as a violation of the criminal statutes. This definition limits the study of crime to only those behaviors for which a person has been caught and convicted. Edwin H. Sutherland, who coined the term *white-collar crime*, offered a modified legalistic definition of crime, describing it as punishable behavior. Thorsten Sellin defined crime as a violation of conduct norms, many of which are not prohibited by law. Hermann Mannheim similarly defined crime as antisocial behavior. Both of these definitions are part of the *normative* definition of crime, the next position on the continuum.

New criminology, also labeled *critical* or *radical* criminology, treats crime and deviance as synonymous. This perspective views the definition of crime as a political and economic process that is controlled by powerful groups in society. New criminologists Herman and Julia Schwendinger define crime based on human rights, which they describe as being such things as food, shelter, and medical care. Crimes under this definition would include racism, sexism, and poverty.

Most criminologists do not favor strict legalistic definitions of crime. Such a definition avoids issues such as discretion and other reactions of the criminal justice system. It ignores many harmful acts, while including many victimless crimes, as it restricts attention to criminalized behaviors.

What behaviors are defined as crime is relative to time, location, and who is doing the defining. Many acts that were once outlawed, such as abortion, are now legal. Other behaviors that were once ignored by the criminal justice system, such as marital rape, are now crimes.

## Paradigms in Criminology

There are five major paradigms, or theoretical perspectives. The *rational choice*, or free will, paradigm views people as rational and focuses on deterrence. The *positivistic* paradigm views crime as being caused by forces that the individual cannot fully control. It has been the dominant theory in American criminology for most of the twentieth century. The *interactionist* paradigm seeks to explain why people are labeled criminal and questions state definitions of crime. *Critical* criminology, including new, radical, and Marxist perspectives, questions state definitions of crime but also questions why the less-powerful segments of society are subject to criminal sanctions more so than the more powerful members. *Integration* combines two or more paradigms in attempt to better explain criminal phenomena.

## Policy and Criminology

The knowledge yielded by criminological inquiry can be valuable independent of any potential application to the crime problem. Theory (efforts to understand and explain crime), however, is fundamental to practicing criminology. Applied programs can only follow the lead provided by theoretical foundations. All theories, though, have practical implications.

Three issues should be considered while studying your text and this study guide: the relativity of crime; the prevalence of the scientific method in criminology; and the impact of ideology.

## Key Terms

**conflict:** a belief that the law disproportionately reflects the interest of a powerful minority within society

**consensus:** agreement among people on what should or should not be crimes

**crime:** viewed differently by criminologists along a continuum; Paul Tappan suggested a highly legalistic definition based on the convicted and punished violation of legal codes; Edwin Sutherland used a modified legalistic definition based on punishable behavior; Thorsten Sellin defined crime as a violation of conduct norms; Herman and Julia Schwendinger prefer a humanistic definition based on human rights

**crime seriousness scales:** a measure of public rankings of crimes by seriousness

**criminologist:** person who studies crime, criminals, and criminal behavior; person who attempts to discover the causes of crime

**criminology:** defined in various ways, but the most elementary and widely accepted definition is the scientific study of crime

**critical criminology:** perspective that focuses on how the power elite defines crime to suit themselves

**gender subordination:** institutionalized exercise of power by males over females

**ideology:** refers to a set of beliefs or values that we all develop, often subconsciously, about the way the world ought to be

**integration:** the combination of two or more paradigms in an attempt to better explain criminal phenomena

**interactionism:** criminological paradigm revolving around the actions and reactions of persons and groups that provides the basis for seeking explanations of why and how persons are labeled criminal

**legalistic definition (of crime):** definition of crime as a punishable violation of criminal law

**methodology:** refers to the techniques or methods that criminologists use to learn facts as they attempt to answer the "whys" of crime

**new criminology:** a term for various conflict explanations of crime

**paradigm:** a broad theoretical orientation or framework for explaining phenomena such as crime

**positivism:** criminological paradigm that assumes that forces beyond the control of individuals determine criminal behavior

**radical criminology:** a general term for various conflict perspectives for explaining crime synonymous with "new" or "critical" criminology

**rational choice:** the view that people are rational and able to make decisions regarding their behavior

**relativity of crime:** the definition of which acts are considered crimes varies by time, place, and who is doing the defining

**scientific method:** an approach to the study of phenomena that incorporates both theory and observations

**theoretical integration:** the combination of two or more theoretical perspectives in an attempt to develop an optimal explanation of crime

**theory:** an effort to explain or make sense of the world

## Key Criminologists

**Hermann Mannheim:** identified all antisocial behavior as falling within the domain of criminological enterprise

**Herman and Julia Schwendinger:** offered a critical definition of crime based on human rights, including racism, sexism, imperialism, and poverty

**Thorsten Sellin:** an important criminologist who defined criminology as the study of violations of conduct norms, only a subset of which are embodied in the criminal law at any given place and time

**Edwin Sutherland:** a renowned American criminologist who defined crime as an act that is punishable; Sutherland introduced the concept of white-collar crime, which subsequently broadened the boundaries of criminology

**Paul Tappan:** offered a strict legalistic definition of crime that excludes behavior that is not criminalized, detected, or reported to law-enforcement authorities and successfully prosecuted, thereby limiting criminological study to convicted offenders

# Chapter 2
# Criminal Law and the Criminal Justice System

## Summary

The study of violations of the criminal law requires a working knowledge of its principles and how they are used by those in the criminal justice system to apply the label of "criminal" to offenders. Knowledge of the criminal justice process contributes to a sound understanding in criminology because that process determines who is and who is not criminalized.

## The Foundation of Criminal Law

There are two general orientations for understanding the criminal law. The first is the consensus perspective, which views the law as the embodiment of social needs and values. Emile Durkheim, who favored this view, described crime as defining the boundaries of acceptable behavior and solidifying society. Thus, crime is actually healthy and functional to society. The conflict perspective views the law as serving the interest of the wealthy and powerful. These two views may be combined. There is evidence that the criminal codes were created to protect the interests of society's powerful elite, but once in effect, the laws protect everyone in society.

What behaviors are defined as crimes is relative to time and location. Examples include abortion, previously outlawed but now legalized, and smoking tobacco, which is now restricted in public areas in many jurisdictions. Vagrancy laws were ruled unconstitutional in the U.S. Supreme Court case of *Papachristou v. Jacksonville* (1972). Although vagrancy statutes had been used most recently for such purposes as holding criminal suspects and controlling "undesirables," they were first created in 1349 to force laborers to work for low wages during a labor shortage caused by the Black Plague.

The United States has passed several laws outlawing various drugs that were once legally available. Laws forbidding computer hacking have also been created in recent years. Tobacco companies have come under attack after acknowledging publicly that tobacco is a harmful drug. However, in *FDA v. Brown & Williamson Tobacco Corp.* (2000), the Supreme Court ruled that the FDA lacked the authority to regulate tobacco and thus would have no choice but to declare tobacco illegal.

Rape can be considered another example. What constitutes rape can vary from one observer to another and from one time period to another. The unusual case of Mary Kay Letourneau, age 34, and Vili Fualaau, age 12, illustrates the issue of relative criminality in a sexual nature. In recent years rape has begun to encompass a wider range of sexual violations and is now considered a gender-neutral crime.

## The Concept of Law

Law is divided into criminal, civil, and administrative components. Crimes may result from forbidden actions or failing to fulfill required actions (commission or omission). Criminal proceedings rest on the premise that the accused has violated the rights of society, or the community at large. Felonies are the most serious crimes, punishable by execution or one year or more of imprisonment. Misdemeanors are subject to incarceration of less than one year, usually in jails. Violations are subject to small fines. Specific elements must be proven in a crime, such as the *actus reus*, or physical element, and the *mens rea*, or intent, and conviction requires "proof beyond a reasonable doubt." Civil law, or torts, address wrongs against individuals rather than crimes against society. Civil law cases may provide compensation to the injured party, but do not involve criminal penalties, and only require a "preponderance of evidence." Administrative law results from a legislative body delegating authority to a regulatory authority, such as the Food and Drug Administration or the Internal Revenue Service. It combines elements of both criminal and civil law.

## Criminology vs. Criminal Justice

The focus of criminology is on explaining crime, while criminal justice is more concerned with societal, and particularly official, reactions to crime and criminals. While criminology tends to be more theoretical and includes explanations that do not have immediate policy implications, criminal justice is more descriptive and is more likely to suggest courses of action for criminal justice practitioners.

## Goals of Criminal Justice

Criminal justice has four goals. *Deterrence* involves the threat of sanctions to scare potential offenders from violating the law. General deterrence involves making an example of the convicted offender to others of the perils of engaging in criminal behavior. Special deterrence involves "teaching the offender a lesson." *Incapacitation* attempts to make an offender incapable of committing further offenses. Incarceration is the most widely used form of incapacitation, but it is not completely incapacitative. The imprisoned offender can victimize correctional staff or other inmates. The only completely incapacitative punishment is execution. *Rehabilitation*, based on a medical model, seeks to change offenders so they no longer desire to commit crimes. *Retribution* is the only goal of criminal justice that cannot be justified on utilitarian grounds. It seeks a moral balance by punishing offenders for past wrongful conduct.

## The Idea and Practice of Criminal Justice

Describing criminal justice as a system suggests that the agencies involved are coordinated and seek common goals. However, the agencies involved are not coordinated very strongly and may seek conflicting goals. The criminal justice funnel refers to the large number of suspected offenders exiting the system at each stage, from criminal offense to punishment. The practice of criminal justice is based on the separation of powers, with each branch of government having control over different segments of its operation. Due process of law is important to American criminal justice, with the Bill of Rights' entrance into criminal law through the Fourteenth Amendment's due process clause.

Policing is predominantly carried out at the local level of government. Innovative new policing strategies have been developed over the years. Policing has also come to be influenced by more college-educated, minority, and female officers. Police executives typically deny the existence of discretion within their departments, insisting that their officers practice full enforcement of the law. In reality, discretion is an integral part of police work. Police departments differ from most organizations in that the use of discretion increases as one moves down through the hierarchy from chief to patrol officer.

The judge, the prosecutor, and the defense attorney comprise the courtroom work group. Although justice is ideally dispensed through adversarial proceedings, most cases are actually disposed through plea bargaining. The courtroom work group has cooperative relationships and typically debates on the appropriate punishment, rather than guilt versus innocence.

Corrections may be institutional, most commonly represented by prisons, or community-based. Community-based corrections are less expensive and contain the great majority of convicted criminal offenders, including probation, parole, and halfway houses. Probation officers serve conflicting roles. They must monitor the offender's behavior for violations and try to facilitate the offender's rehabilitation. Probation officers also write pre-sentence investigation reports to be used in setting the offender's sentence and guide those who are involved in his or her treatment.

## Gender and the Administration of Justice

Discretion plays an important role in all parts of the criminal justice process. Criminology gave little serious attention to female offenders until recently. Most studies have concluded that the criminal justice system treats women less harshly than men. While there may be legally relevant reasons for this difference in treatment based on gender, chivalry and paternalism have been offered as an explanation by most criminologists studying this phenomenon. Another theory has been that women are subjected to more informal social control than men and are therefore thought to require less formal social control. However, juvenile girls have been treated much more harshly when committing status offenses, such as running away from home.

## Key Terms

*actus reus:* "guilty act," or the physical element in a crime; it is comprised of conduct that is prohibited or of failure to act in a manner required by the criminal

**administrative law:** laws based on the delegation of rule-making authority from a legislative body to a regulatory body

**adversarial process:** process by which issues are settled in a court of law

**chivalry:** belief that women are not really capable of serious crime and that men should serve as protectors of females

**civil law:** also known as *torts*, civil law violations are noncriminal legal wrongs against individuals

**community-based corrections:** a wide array of programs operated within a community setting to rehabilitate and monitor offenders

**conflict:** an orientation that views the criminal law as operating in the interest of a wealthy and powerful elite whose desires conflict with those of members of less privileged groups

**consensus:** an orientation that views the criminal law as developing and operating in the interest of society at large

**courtroom work group prohibition:** the prosecutor, the defense attorney, and the judge

**criminal justice process:** the steps or phases through which suspected criminals may pass in the criminal justice system

**criminal justice system:** a collection of agencies that collectively administer justice including police, prosecutors, courts, and corrections

**criminal law:** legal codes that politically define which violations of conduct norms are crimes

**deterrence:** the use of punitive sanctions to dissuade persons from committing criminal offenses in the future

**due process of law:** embodiment of the Bill of Rights; enters into criminal law via the Fourteenth Amendment

**Eighteenth Amendment:** mandated prohibition (1920 until 1933); failure, by most measures

**ethnocentrism:** believing that the customs and values of one's own culture are superior to any other culture

**evil women:** women who violate gender-role expectations; should be punished harshly

**felony:** the most serious type of offense, punishable by execution or incarceration for one year or more

**furlough:** unescorted temporary releases from prison

**gateway drug:** drug that acts as a stepping stone to later use of hard drugs

**general deterrence:** serves as an example to others to prevent criminality

**Harrison Act (1914):** criminalized the sale and possession of opiates

**incapacitation:** goal of criminal justice that seeks to reduce or to eliminate the capacity of offenders to commit additional crimes, most commonly by confining in prison

**just deserts:** goal of criminal justice that involves the punishment of past wrongdoing in order to achieve a moral balance; also known as *retribution*

**Marijuana Tax Act (1937):** legislation that made the failure to pay an exorbitant tax on marijuana an offense, effectively outlawing its possession

***mens rea:*** "guilty mind," or the mental element of crime generally termed *intent*

**misdemeanor:** offenses that are punishable by incarceration in jail for a period up to 11 months and 29 days

**moral entrepreneurship:** campaigning for laws rooted in moral conceptions, most often calling for criminalization of crimes without specific victims

**moral panics:** campaigns of misinformation; exaggerated responses to such concerns as witchcraft, child abuse, communism, or alcohol

*nolle prosequi:* prosecutor's discretionary power to not prosecute

**parole:** the release of an inmate from prison to serve the remainder of the sentence under supervision in the community

**plea bargaining:** process by which the defense agrees to plead guilty in exchange for the prosecution's recommendation for a specific punishment, thereby avoiding trial

**police discretion:** selection of particular responses from among an array of alternatives that is inevitable in and fundamental to police work, although police administrators typically deny its existence

**post-penetration rape:** occurs when a woman initially consents to sexual intercourse but withdraws the consent during the act, but the male partner refuses to immediately end the activity

**probation:** the most widely employed form of community corrections; entails serving a sentence in the community under specified conditions and with supervision by a probation officer

**Prohibition:** the period of time from 1920-1933 when alcohol was prohibited in the United States

**Rape Shield laws:** impose limits on the ability of the defense to question the history and character of the alleged victim

**rehabilitation:** changing offenders by removing the motivation to engage in criminal behavior

**relativity of law:** the variation in content of criminal codes across time and places

**retribution:** goal of criminal justice that involves the punishment of past wrongdoing in order to achieve a moral balance; also known as *just deserts*

**Sentencing Reform Act (1984):** legislation that created the U.S. Sentencing Commission, which developed sentencing guidelines specifying sentence range by offense and offender type

**separation of powers:** distinct roles of each of the three branches of U.S. government (executive, legislative, judicial) relative to criminal justice operations

**sodomy:** "victimless" crime usually defined as a sexual act that involves one person's sex organs and another person's mouth or anus; it is often enforced against homosexuals

**specific (or special) deterrence:** serves to "teach a lesson" to the offender to prevent recidivism

**unintended consequences (of prohibition):** increased consumption of distilled spirits (relative to beer); provided organized crime with opportunities

**victimless crime:** crime in which there is no complaining victim

## Key Criminologists

**Meda Chesney-Lind:** a leading feminist criminologist who has noted that the behavioral problems of girls have been sexualized, while those of boys have not

**John Curra:** wrote *The Relativity of Crime*; proponent of theory that behavior that is laudable in one instance may be labeled criminal in another instance

**Emile Durkheim:** an eighteenth-century sociologist who viewed the law as formalizing the norms and mores of the community, thus developing and operating in the interest of society at large

**Cesare Lombroso:** nineteenth-century Italian physician who adopted a social Darwinian perspective; developed the concept of atavism; first person to apply scientific principles to the study of criminals

**Otto Pollak:** introduced notion of masked criminality; believed women engage in considerable amounts of crime but it went undiscovered because of women's secrecy, deceitfulness, and chivalry

# Chapter 3
# Production of Crime Statistics

## Summary

There are three major sources of quantitative data on crime. The Uniform Crime Reports (UCR) is comprised of data collected by the Federal Bureau of Investigation (FBI) from police departments. The National Crime Victimization Surveys (NCVS) consist of information gathered from victims of crimes. Self-report surveys contain data collected from criminal offenders. In addition to these quantitative data sources, there are observational studies that provide valuable descriptive information, but may lack validity and reliability.

## Review of Elementary Research Methodology

There are different levels of explanation of crime causation. Macro-level explanations relate to crime rates. The micro level attempts to explain why individuals commit crime. The dependent variable is the thing that the researcher is seeking to explain; the independent variable is the thing that the researcher thinks will explain the dependent variable.

Generalizability, the ability to make inferences about groups other than those studied, is gained through sound research design and sampling procedures. In the classic experimental design, the experimental group receives a treatment and the control group is not treated. However, the experimental design usually cannot be used for criminological studies. Criminological studies may use comparison groups or statistical controls to try to generalize results. Cross-sectional research designs, such as public opinion polls, collect information only once about some specific topic. Longitudinal research designs gather data across time, allowing historical changes to be examined and correct temporal ordering of variables to be determined. Probability sampling should be used to increase generalizability.

To prove that an independent variable causes a dependent variable (causality) requires three criteria. The two variables must be correlated. The independent variable must occur before the dependent variable. Any other possible causes must be controlled.

## History of Official Crime Statistics

When the U.S. Department of Justice was created in 1870, Congress mandated that crime statistics be reported annually. Though this did not materialize at the time, currently more than 18,000 police agencies report crime data to the FBI. These agencies represent approximately 95 percent of the U.S. population. The UCR are divided into two parts. The eight crimes in Part I, known as *Index*, are criminal homicide, forcible rape, robbery, aggravated assault, burglary, larceny-theft, motor vehicle theft, and arson. Some serious crimes, such as kidnapping and white-collar offenses, are not included in the Index because they do not occur often enough or are not reported to the police often enough to create an accurate database. Media reports of crime rates (the amount of crime per 100,000 population) are derived from the Index. Part II of the UCR contains crimes that are considered nonserious and cover only crimes that result in an arrest. The UCR also contain data such as where crimes occur, injuries, monetary losses, the personal characteristics of victims and offenders, and information about police agencies. Although reporting statistics to the FBI remains voluntary, agencies that do not contribute to the UCR are viewed "unprofessional."

Of course, the UCR does not include information about crimes of which the police are unaware, but the data that it does include are easily accessible and allow for comparisons across time and location. However, there are some reporting problems because different agencies report crime statistics based on varying definitions.

## Alternative Measures of Crime

Self-report studies have been used mostly with juvenile subjects. One of the most sophisticated self-report studies is the National Youth Survey (NYS), which began in 1977. NYS collected data on the same cohort nine times annually until 1981 and then five additional times in the following years. There are currently several other self-report studies being conducted, including one by the National Institute of Justice and the John D. and Catherine T. MacArthur Foundation and three sponsored by the Office of Juvenile Justice and Delinquency Prevention (OJJDP). Self-report studies are intended to measure the dark figure of crime not reported in the UCR. They are not subject to political manipulation. There are several criticisms of self-report studies. There have been very few studies of adult populations, and those that have included adults have mostly been limited to prisoners. Most of the studies emphasize status offenses. There are also methodological problems, including sampling, selective loss, falsification, validity, reliability, memory decay, and interviewer measurement error issues.

The National Crime Victimization Survey (NCVS) was begun in 1972, consisting of both a sample of American cities and a national sample. It contains information gathered from persons over the age of 12 years and is conducted by the U.S. Bureau of Census. Information collected in this survey includes respondents' views on fear of crime, the perceived decline or improvement of the neighborhood in regard to crime, and steps that have been taken to protect the household against victimization. Among other advantages of the NCVS is that a lot of information is collected about relatively few crimes. The UCR, on the other hand, collects a little information about a lot of crimes. However, caution must be exercised when interpreting NCVS data, as problems include those common to self-report studies: falsification, telescoping, validity, interviewer effect, and sampling. Another problem with this household-respondent method is underreporting of the amount of crime.

In part because of the number of criticisms against the UCR, the National Incident-Based Reporting System (NIBRS) was introduced in 1984 to enhance the quality, quantity, and timeliness of crime statistical data collected by the law enforcement community and to improve the methodology used for compiling, analyzing, auditing, and publishing the collected crime data. This system classifies crimes into Group A (22 offenses) and Group B (11 offenses) and includes crime circumstances, victim and offender information, arrestee data, and information about the extent of damage to both person and property.

## Comparison of UCR, SRD, and NCVS Data Source

The UCR report an increase in crime between 1960 and 1990 but suggest that crime has been declining since 1991. The NCVS and self-report data (SRD) indicate that crime has remained stable or even decreased. The NCVS and SRD measure actual behavior; the UCR measures police response. Given the different measurements, it is possible that each source is correct in its own particular way.

## Other Measures of Crime

There are other types of measures of crime. Cohort studies gather information about the criminal behavior of groups of people as they age. The Philadelphia study by Marvin Wolfgang, Thorsten Sellin, and Robert Figlio covering a cohort born in 1945 revealed that 35 percent of the boys had police contact prior to age 18; approximately 6 percent of the boys were responsible for about half of all contacts with police; and race and social class were correlated with police contact.

Descriptive biographies gather detailed information on the criminal behavior of one person. While biographies have many generalizability problems, they are useful exploratory research and lead to hypotheses for more systematic study.

Observational studies are used to gather information about criminal offenders in their natural settings. Criminologists must consider several ethical questions before engaging in observational studies, such as whether to report observed illegal activities and guaranteeing confidentiality. Observational studies also suffer from generalization issues.

## Key Terms

**biographies:** a methodology for studying criminals by collecting detailed information about one individual and his or her criminal lifestyle

**causality:** The difficult process of ascertaining what causes what; for example, before it can be said that poverty causes crime, three criteria need to be met: (1) it must be shown that the variables are correlated; (2) temporal ordering must be established (the independent variable must come before the dependent variable); and (3) rival or potential explanatory factors need to be controlled

**cohort studies:** a research methodology that follows the same group of individuals as they age to study changes over time

**comparison group:** a group that is similar to the experimental group and can be contrasted to understand causality

**control group**: the group in an experiment that receives no treatment and is compared to the one that does

**correlation:** as one variable changes, the other variable also changes

**crime frequency:** refers to the number of offenses that occur in a given population during a specified time interval

**crime prevalence:** refers to the number of persons in a population that report one or more offenses of a given type within a specified period

**crime rate:** the rate of crimes to some population unit; the Uniform Crime Reports, for example, report the number of crimes per 100,000 population

**crime seriousness scale:** a measurement of public rankings of crimes by seriousness

**cross-sectional design:** collect data at one time point about some specified issue and period

**dark figure of crime:** the percentage of unknown crimes; many crimes are never reported to the police

**dependent variable:** the phenomenon to be explained

**experimental group:** the group in an experiment that receives the treatment

**hierarchical rule:** Uniform Crime Reports (UCR) instructions mandating that a crime be tabulated in the most serious category

**independent variable:** the explanation for the dependent variable or the variable influencing or acting upon others

**Index crimes:** UCR Part I crimes, considered to be particularly serious. The eight Index crimes are criminal homicide, forcible rape, robbery, aggravated assault, burglary, larceny-theft, motor vehicle theft, and arson

**levels of explanation:** the macro level attempts to explain crime rates; the micro level seeks to understand why individuals commit crimes

**longitudinal designs:** collect information across time, allowing for examination of historical changes and for establishing correct temporal ordering of variables

**macro level:** level of explanation that attempts to explain crime rates

**micro level:** level of explanation that attempts to explain why individuals commit crime

**National Crime Survey:** the nation's primary source of information on crime victimization, including frequency, characteristics, and consequences of criminal victimization in the United States

**observational studies:** allows the researcher to become established in and observe law-breaking groups in their natural settings

**Part I crimes:** synonymous with Index crimes

**Part II crimes:** include most other crimes not itemized in Part I (Index offenses) of the UCR; 20 specific crimes and a catchall "other" category are in this section

**probability sample:** this means that every subject or case to which one hopes to be able to generalize has an equal probability of being selected for inclusion in the study

**reliability:** whether the research results are accurate

**self-report studies:** request individuals to indicate the type and amount of criminal behavior in which they have engaged

**stratified probability sample:** divides the population into appropriate categories and then samples within these strata

**telescoping:** projecting an event outside the time period being studied

**Uniform Crime Reports (UCR):** consist of information collected by local police departments and forwarded to the FBI

**validity:** whether the research design is measuring the desired phenomenon

**victimization surveys:** ask respondents to indicate the types of crimes in which they have been victims

## Key Criminologists

**Albert D. Biderman:** a criminologist who concluded that once the different methodologies of the UCR, NCVS, and SDR are considered, the findings are not as disparate as it appears

**Delbert Elliott:** with his colleagues at the University of Colorado, is conducting the National Youth Survey (NYS), a self-report study of delinquency based on a probability sample of youth in the continental United States

**James Garofalo:** with Michael Hindelang, studied whether victims would report a victimization to an unknown interviewer

**Michael Hindelang:** with James Garofalo, studied whether victims would report a victimization to an unknown interviewer

**David Huizinga:** is conducting a longitudinal research project utilizing self-report data to examine the causes and correlates of delinquency in high-risk neighborhoods, including children as young as seven in the samples to allow for a better determination of early life experiences associated with delinquent or problem behavior

**Rolf Loeber:** participated in research project; utilized self-report data to examine causes of delinquency in high-risk neighborhoods

**F. Ivan Nye:** with James F. Short, Jr., found that parents' socioeconomic background and the quality of family life were not related to delinquency, but the study had several methodological problems

**Stephen W. Raudenbush:** along with Robert Sampson, participated in the Project on Human Development in Chicago Neighborhoods (PHDCN)

**Robert J. Sampson:** along with Stephen Raudenbush, participated in the Project on Human Development in Chicago Neighborhoods (PHDCN)

**Thorsten Sellin:** warned about depending upon court and prison records in studying crime, stating that the value of crime statistics decreases as one becomes further removed from the crime itself; with Marvin Wolfgang and

Robert Figlio, Sellin was involved in the Philadelphia Study, which looked at a cohort of all males born in Philadelphia in 1945 who lived in the city continuously from age 10 through 18 (9,945 boys)

**James F. Short, Jr.:** with F. Ivan Nye, found that parents' socioeconomic background and the quality of family life were not related to delinquency, although several methodological questions have been raised

**Terence P. Thornberry:** is conducting a longitudinal research project utilizing self-report data to examine the causes and correlates of delinquency in high-risk neighborhoods

Chapter 4
# Distribution of Crime

---

## Summary

Explaining criminal causation requires knowledge of who is committing crime, who is being victimized, and when and where crime is occurring. It is also important to know about the number and types of crimes.

## Volume of Crime: Uniform Crime Reports

The Uniform Crime Reports (UCR) recorded nearly 12 million Index crimes in 2004, over 88 percent of which were property crimes and less than 12 percent of which were violent crimes. The crime rate was almost 40 Index offenses per 1,000 people living in the United States. Approximately 11.7 million arrests were made in 2004 for UCR Part II offenses. Because the UCR only records crimes that come to the attention of police, the actual amount of crime is higher than these figures. Louise Shelley reports that developing countries experience rural violence and urban property crimes, while developed countries with larger urban populations have higher rates of property offences. Crime rates in the United States generally exceed that of other developed countries by several times. Though the disparity is rates has lessened, violent crime in the U.S. remains well above average.

The southern states had the highest rates of murder, rape, and assault, while the western states have the highest rate of auto theft. Overall, crime rates are highest in the southern and western states. Regarding the size of communities, cities and towns outside Metropolitan Statistical Areas (MSAs) have the highest crime rates, followed by MSAs. Rural areas have the lowest crime rates.

Although the UCR report that crimes occur at a rather steady rate throughout the year, there are fewer crimes during January and February and more crimes during July, August, and December. The lower crime rates in winter months is probably due to people staying home more and thus reducing the number of available targets for crime. Conversely, the higher crime crates in the summer and likely due to people being out of their home, making them more available for victimization. The high crime rates in

December are likely due to pressures related to the holiday season. Most crimes occur during the evening and at night. More crimes are committed on weekends than during the week.

The UCR suggests that crime rates rose until 1980, fell until 1984, increased again until 1991, and then dropped suddenly. Criminologists had expected the decrease in crime rates in the 1980s based on members of the baby boom aging out of the crime-prone ages of 18–23.

## Volume of Crime: National Crime Victimization Survey

The National Crime Victimization Survey (NCVS) reports higher crime rates than the UCR. The NCVS recorded more than 24.2 million crimes for 2004, 77.1 percent of which were property crimes and 21.9 percent of which were violent offenses. The NCVS reports victimization rates that are almost five times higher than those suggested by the UCR. Correlations between the reporting of crimes in the UCR and the NCVS have been found to be higher for theft crimes such as motor vehicle theft, robbery, and burglary than for violent crimes such as rape and aggravated assault. The NCVS, similar to the UCR, reports more crimes committed in cities than in rural areas. The NCVS indicates that, except for rape, more crimes are committed on the street than in the victim's home. The NCVS data also agree with the UCR data that, except for rape, most crimes are committed at night.

## Volume of Crime: Self-Report Studies

Self-report data (SRD) cannot be directly compared to the UCR or NCVS because the only national studies so far have involved only juveniles and young adults. SDR report crime rates two ways. A prevalence rate is the proportion of the population that reports committing a particular offence. A frequency rate, also called *individual offending rate* or *lambda*, is the number of crimes reported as occurring in a population during a specific time period. The National Youth Survey (NYS) has offered the best self-report data based on a national sample. The NYS involved annual interviews of the same youths beginning in 1977. According to NYS data from 1980, 65 percent of the youths surveyed aged 15 to 21 had committed at least one delinquent offense. The frequency rate was an average of 32 offenses per person. The NYS data suggest many more offenses were committed than were recorded in the UCR.

While the NYS data show that urban youth commit offenses at a higher rate than rural youths, the difference is not statistically significant. The data from 1977 to 1981 indicate a fairly stable prevalence rate. However, frequency rates during this same time period rose from 19 in 1976 to 32 in 1980. These changes may be due to changes in the cohort and "maturation effects."

## Distribution of Crime by Gender

Criminology has traditionally concentrated solely on the behavior of males. Females have been excluded from studies partly because official arrest records indicate that few women commit crime. It has also been assumed that the crimes committed by women are primarily sexual in nature. Studies of female criminality increased in the 1970s. Recent hypotheses on female crime suggest that girls are socialized differently than boys, resulting in females having less access to illegitimate opportunities. Given the lack of freedom, opportunity, and training, fewer women become serious offenders. However, in 2004, females comprised 28 percent of the arrests for Index crimes. Female arrest rates also increased significantly more than arrest rates for males between 1973 and 2004. The increase in arrests of females has been linked to the women's liberation movement's removing the difference in role expectations between men and women. The power-control model of delinquency suggests that females are subject to more informal control than males, and delinquency occurs in the presence of power and absence of control.

Girls are more likely to be sexually abused than boys. Girls are also typically abused at an earlier age and for a longer period of time than are boys. Most girls in the criminal justice system have been physically abused and entered the criminal justice system for running away from home. Imprisoned adult women also have been found very often to have been physically or sexually abused as children.

UCR data indicate that just over 76 percent of all arrests in 2004 were of males. For Index arrests, nearly 72 percent were of males. Females appear to be arrested primarily for property offenses. Males are arrested at a higher rate than females for all crimes except prostitution and runaway. While NCVS data indicate different crime rates than the UCR, both data sets show a similar proportion of male and female offenders for crimes of violence. Information on property offenders is not available because victims usually do not see the offenders. Self-report data show more females committing crime than either the UCR or NCVS. SRD also indicate that the criminality of women is similar to that of men but occurs less frequently.

## Distribution of Crime by Age

UCR data indicate that people under the age of 22 commit slightly less than 43 percent of Index crimes. NCVS data indicate a similar distribution. Both the UCR and NYS show that criminality increases through adolescence, peaking at about age 16 or 17.

The concept of criminal careers compares engaging in criminal activity to other occupations. Selective incapacitation of career criminals (habitual offenders) has been suggested to reduce the amount of crime. Michael Gottfredson and Travis Hirschi oppose the criminal career paradigm. Insisting that criminal behavior is caused by low self-control, they maintain that the decline in criminal activity that is typical in individuals after age 16 or 17 is due to maturational reform rather than an effect of age.

## Distribution of Crime by Race

Both UCR and NCVS data indicate that African-Americans are responsible for a disproportionate amount of crime. However, the NYS and most other self-report data do not show any racial difference in crime rates. Although 37 percent of all arrests for Index offenses are of African-Americans, only 15 percent of the American population is African-American. There may be some differential enforcement occurring, with African-Americans more likely to be arrested than whites.

## Distribution of Crime by Social Class

It is difficult to define social class. The definition is usually based on education, income, and occupation, but these variables are hard to measure. While many criminologists assume that lower-class persons commit a disproportionate amount of crime, the actual relationship between social class and involvement in delinquent behavior is unclear.

## Victims of Crime

According to the NCVS, slightly more than one out of every six households was victimized in 2004. Household theft is most likely for households with incomes greater than $75,000. Households with incomes of less than $7,500 have the greatest likelihood of experiencing violent, property, burglary, and personal crimes, specifically rape/sexual assault, aggravated assault, and robbery. Urban households have the greatest victimization rates, while rural households have the lowest rates. Hispanic households are most likely to be victimized, followed by African-American households. White households are the least likely to experience victimizations. Larger households are more likely to be victimized than single-person households. As males are significantly more likely to commit crime, they are also more often victimized than females. Teenagers are the most likely to experience personal crime, while, contrary to popular opinion, the elderly are the least likely to be victims of crime.

## Key Terms

**age and crime:** shown by research to be very closely related; age is one of the best predictors of law violation, with younger ages (18-23) considered "crime prone"

**career criminal:** synonymous with "habitual offender"

**criminal career:** assumes that criminal activity is similar to other occupations, with a beginning, a period of activity, and an ending of the career; the criminal career literature is largely an outgrowth of prediction models and the attempt to identify the costs of crime relative to the costs of incarceration

**escalation:** an increase in the seriousness of offending

**frequency rates:** also called *individual offending rates* or *lambda*; refer to the number of offenses that occur in a given population during a specified time interval; they may be expressed as an average number of offenses per person or as the number of offenses per some population base, comparable to the UCR and NCVS data

**gender and crime:** shown by research to be closely related, with the male gender serving as the best single predictor of law violation; this raises many interesting issues, such as gender socialization patterns

**geographical crime distribution:** crime rates tend to be higher in the southern and western states; crime rates are also higher in metropolitan statistical areas (MSAs) than in non-MSAs

**individual offending rates:** frequency rates for individuals' offending; sometimes called *lambda*

**initiation:** the onset or beginning of a criminal career

**lambda:** frequency or individual offending rates

**maturation effects:** as they age, persons begin to engage in different types of behavior

**power-control theory:** theory that the presence of power and the absence of control create conditions in which delinquency can occur; used to explain why women commit less delinquency than men

**prevalence rates:** refer to the number of persons in a population that report one or more offenses of a given type within a specified period; the prevalence rate is typically expressed as a proportion of persons in the population who have reported some involvement in a particular offense or set of offenses; prevalence rates are informative, indicating the number of different persons involved in criminal acts

**race and crime:** the common notion is that African-Americans and some other minorities are over-represented in crime statistics; this does appear to be the case when we examine UCR data; the NCVS data also show a disproportionate number of perceived offenders to be African-America; most of the self-report studies, however, (including the NYS) do not find any differences in crime rate by race

**selective incapacitation:** the incarceration of career criminals and other high rate offenders in order to reduce societal costs (e.g., economic and personal injury costs)

**social class and crime:** although neither UCR nor NCVS provide information about the perpetrator's social class, the common assumption has been that members of the lower class commit a disproportionate share of all crimes; however, self-report data provide contradictory evidence on this matter

**temporal crime distribution:** there are slightly fewer crimes in January and February, and slightly more crimes in July, August, and December; the prevalence of crime is also higher in the evening and nighttime hours and over the weekend

**termination:** the cessation of criminal activity in a criminal career

**underclass:** the portion of the population outside the mainstream of the American occupational system

**victimization:** the process of becoming a victim of crime; various characteristics are associated with that probability

## Key Criminologists

**Freda Adler:** insists that we should study nations not obsessed with crime in order to determine what socio-cultural factors tend to inhibit criminal activity; she also connected the rise in female crime with the rise in women's assertiveness brought about by the women's movement and predicted that female crime would begin to resemble male crime

**Alfred Blumstein:** a vocal proponent of the criminal career paradigm

**John Braithwaite:** a well-known Australian criminologist whose research on social class and crime revealed an inverse relationship (i.e., the lower the social class, the more criminal activity)

**Meda Chesney-Lind:** a leading feminist criminologist who has been critical of the women's liberation-crime relationship, likening it to the moral panic associated with past witch hunts that sought to enforce appropriate female sex roles; for Chesney-Lind, the liberation and crime debate provided a deflection of the general hostility toward the women's movement away from women, as a group, onto the female offenders

**Michael Gottfredson:** working with Travis Hirschi, is an outspoken opponent of the value of the criminal career paradigm; they believe that criminal behavior is a result of low self-control

**John Hagan:** working with Ronald Simpson and John Gillis, used a power-control model of delinquency to explain why girls commit less delinquency

**Travis Hirschi:** wrote *Causes of Delinquency* (1969), in which he spelled out his version of social control theory; working with Michael Gottredson, Hirschi is an outspoken opponent of the value of the criminal career paradigm; they believe that criminal behavior is a result of low self-control

**Steven Messner:** worked with Richard Rosenfeld, examining the fluctuations in crime rates over time, including homicide rates and robbery rates

**Richard Rosenfeld:** worked with Steven Messner, examining the fluctuations in crime rates over time

**Rita Simon:** in *The Contemporary Woman in Crime* (1975), examined the statistical picture of female crime over a number of decades; she concluded that some types of crimes (predominately white-collar offenses) will increase, while other types (violent crimes, in particular) will decrease because of the change in the position of women in society

**Darrell Steffensmeier:** a criminologist widely known for his research on gender and other correlates of crime; he urged caution in how we interpret changes in female offending, pointing out that the base rate of female offending was extremely small, so even a small change strongly affects the total percentage; his research on the aging of members of the baby book suggested that this accounted for 40 percent of the decrease in crime rates between 1980 and 1984

**Charles Tittle:** criminologist whose research contributed to empirical and conceptual clarity in the early phases of contemporary deterrence research; he has conducted extensive research and testing of the differential association model proposed by Edwin Sutherland; his research has focused on the deficiencies in the causal framework set out by Sutherland; a chief opponent of labeling theory; Tittle claims that propositions of the labeling perspective are not clearly identified so as to allow for empirical research, and believes the theory to be too vague

**William Wilbanks:** in a comprehensive review of the literature, concluded that it is a myth that the criminal justice system is racist, but acknowledged that individual cases of prejudice and discrimination occur

Chapter 5
# Deterrence and Rational Choice Theories of Crime

## Summary

One of the most debated issues when seeking to explain crime is the role of choice and whether decision making on the part of criminals is a rational process. Crime was once understood to be a supernatural phenomenon of demons and witches prior to the emergence of classical thinking. The pre-classical era can be divided into two broad time frames. Before the state injected itself into social control, it was up to each individual or his or her clan to respond to encroachment on his or her rights. There was nothing in early days that approached formal systems of criminal justice. Revenge served to placate and sometimes to compensate victims of crime. Ultimately, however, this led to the dysfunctional cycle of revenge known as *blood feuds*. Thus, the Church and State assumed the role of administration of justice in the Middle Ages, leading to the horrible era of the Holy Inquisition that persisted to the late eighteenth century. It was a period marked by cruel and arbitrary punishment and torture with no protection against false accusations.

## Classical Criminology

The classical school of criminology emerged in reaction to this state of affairs. It was part and parcel of the Enlightenment, seeking to supplant divine rights of royalty and unlimited power of the church with rationalism, intellectualism, and humanitarianism. Cesare Beccaria, often considered the father of classical criminology, concisely stated the principles of classicism in *On Crimes and Punishments* (1764). It was based on the assumption that people are rational, have free will, and are hedonistic. Crime, therefore, can be prevented by credible threats of sanctions. Success in preventing crime is a function of certainty, severity, and celerity of punishment. Cruel and arbitrary punishments were replaced with more humane responses and procedural protection. This is a utilitarian philosophy ("greatest happiness principle") as emphasized by Jeremy Bentham.

Classical thinking provided the foundation for emergence of modern criminal justice system s in the Western world. Both criminal law and procedure were altered to coincide with the assumption of people as rational actors. Each phase of the justice process was also modified in a manner consistent with classical premises as well. Penology became much more humane, while policing became deterrence-based. Sir Robert Peel began the London Metropolitan Police Act of 1829, which established deterrence of crime via random patrol as the primary rationale for policing.

## Contemporary Deterrence Theory

Belief and disbelief in deterrence theory tend to be highly ideological. From early in the twentieth century until the 1960s or 1970s, it was unconditionally rejected by the criminological community, while unconditionally accepted by criminal justice practitioners. Both faiths are reflected in the tiger prevention fallacy and the warden's survey. Beginning in the late 1960s, however, deterrence has been subjected to both empirical and conceptual scrutiny. A careful distinction is now drawn between general deterrence, directed at the community in general, and specific or special deterrence, aimed at preventing a particular offender from repeating their offense(s).

The tipping level is the point at which punishment reaches the minimum level to become operative. Absolute deterrence would be the complete deterrence of everyone, but marginal, partial, or restrictive deterrence recognizes that variations are possible. A deterrent effect may, for example, occur, but crime will be displaced or shifted to other times, locales, or forms.

Extralegal or informal sanctions have come to be viewed by most criminologists as holding more deterrent effects than formal sanctions of the criminal justice system. A considerable amount of research has shown that the shame and embarrassment of being exposed as a deviant to friends and relatives is far more threatening than official punishments, though the formal sanction may serve as the triggering device for informal sanctions. Moreover, as criminologists such as John Braithwaite argue, shaming may serve to build moral awareness or shape one's conscience.

Deterrent effects vary by both type of crime and person. Crimes are more deterrable if rational, instrumental, nonviolent *mala prohibita*, and typically committed in public locations. Study of specific offenses reveal that appreciable deterrent effects may be operative for illegally parking professors on college campuses (Chambliss, 1966) or for cheating college students (Tittle & Rowe, 1973). The Minneapolis Domestic Assault Study also showed strong special deterrent effects when subjecting male assaulters to arrest, but these findings failed to hold up consistently when replicated in six other cities. While deterrent effects continued to be observed for some types of offenders, arrests actually increased recidivism among socially marginal populations such as the unemployed. As the five crime criteria suggest, limited evidence of the deterrability of drunk driving emerges from the research. Some scholars have concluded, however, particularly from examination of cross-cultural evidence, that the sanctions may have an effect of moral education. Consistent with the irrational nature of drunk driving, virtually no support has been found for deterrent effects of capital punishment. Conversely, some support has been found for a brutalization effect whereby violent crime increases following an execution.

Individuals may be more deterrable if they have a low commitment to crime as a way of life, are amateurs, have a lot of potential gain at stake, are older, and are from a higher social class. They also may be more deterrable if their personality is authoritarian, that of a nonrisk-taker, a pessimist, deliberate, and future-oriented. While race and gender may be important factors in deterrability, the research evidence on the direction of their effect is mixed. At one end of the continuum developed by Greg Pogarsky are the *incorrigible*, or those who are not affected by the threats of punishment. At the other end lie *acute conformists*, individuals who require not threat of punishment to compel conformity because other forces prevent them from violating the rules. Additionally, crimes may also be ranked along a continuum from most to least deterrable.

## Rational Choice and Routine Activities

Several different concepts can be found within the deterrence perspective. Beccaria argued that for people to be deterred they must be rational. The contemporary thought on deterrence provided for the rational choice theory, which expands conventional deterrence research by adding several more variables into the reasoning process. It also considers the choices made by the potential offenders and those choices made by those who may become the victims. Consistent with this concept is *target hardening*, or steps one can take to minimize risk of victimization.

In 1979 Lawrence Cohen and Marcus Felson introduced the routine activities or lifestyle approach. Here it is argued that choices made on the part of the potential victims may create or curtail the opportunities for a motivated offender. Routine activities theory originally was not a theory of crime, but a theoretical perspective used to understand victimization. For this reason, three premises are at the core of the theory (the "crime triangle"). First, it is assumed that there are motivated offenders. Second, there must be a suitable target, and finally there is an absence of capable guardians. This theory was originally intended to account for increases in crime because certain social changes facilitated an increase in suitable targets. Only recently have theorists begun to examine the motivated offenders within this theory, as their presence was initially taken for granted.

## Key Terms

**absence of capable guardians:** neither persons nor other agents are present to protect property

**absolute deterrence:** total prevention of crime through threats of punishment

**acute conformists:** people who do not require threats of punishment to compel conformity

**anti-rehabilitation movement:** a popular belief in the 1970s that correctional efforts had failed to significantly reduce recidivism rates (repeat offenses)

**base rate fallacy:** ignoring or underestimating the expected level of punishment

**blood feuding:** the uncontrolled seeking of revenge by kinship groups for perceived wrongdoing by others during the preclassical period preceding placement of the justice process under state control

**bounded rationality:** the idea that limits are imposed on rationality across individual characteristics

**brutalization effect:** the psychological reduction of value in human life that may follow executions or other highly visible violence, resulting in escalation of violent behavior

**certainty, severity, and celerity:** three key variables for the delivery of punishment to achieve deterrent effects; a certain level of each, listed in order of priority, is thought necessary under deterrence theory to achieve a deterrent effect

**classical criminology:** the first natural explanation of crime, rooted in premises of the rationality of humans and the consequent deterrent effect of threats of sanctions; this school of thought has had dramatic impact on the administration of justice in the Western world

**crime displacement:** shifting crime perpetration to different times, locations, or forms rather than abstaining; the net deterrent is crimes prevented minus crimes displaced

**crime triangle:** the three premises at the heart of the routine activities theory: motivated offenders, suitable targets, and absence of capable guardians

**criminogenic:** crime-enhancing

**deterrable:** capable of being stopped or deterred; those affected by threats of punishment

**deterrence theory:** theory that crime can be reduced through threats of sanctions

**embarrassment:** loss of respect in the eyes of others

**Enlightenment:** the historical period in eighteenth-century Europe marked by a shift from emphasizing divine rights of royalty to an emphasis on rationality, intellectualism, and humanitarianism; this provided the backdrop for emergence of the classical school of criminology

**expressive crimes:** offenses motivated by the immediate pleasure of crime

**free will:** freedom to make choices that are not determined by prior causes

**general deterrence:** sanctions aimed at deterring crime among persons other than those who are punished; it is punishing one party as an example for others

**hedonistic:** behavior of someone seeking to increase pleasure and/or reduce pain

**Holy Inquisition:** religious persecution during the Middle Ages in Europe, characterized by torture and arbitrariness; the Enlightenment and emergence of classical criminology were in reaction to these atrocities

**incorrigible:** people not significantly affected by threats of punishment

**instrumental crimes:** offenses motivated by desire for other gains such as the acquisition of property

**justice model:** an anti-rehabilitation movement of the 1970s that saw retribution as the most fundamental goal of a sound justice system

**London Metropolitan Police Act:** organized the first modern police department in 1829 based on the principles of deterrence

*mala in se:* an act considered inherently evil and consequently less responsive to efforts to control through threats of sanctions

*mala prohibita:* an act that is not inherently evil but is prohibited for other reasons, and thus controlled only through threats of sanction

**marginal deterrence:** the prevention of some, but not all, crime through threats of sanctions; also called *restrictive deterrence*

**Minneapolis Domestic Violence Experiment:** assault study; an important policing experiment in the early 1980s that responded to misdemeanor domestic assaults in different ways, finding a deterrent effect for arrests

**motivated offenders:** offenders who commit crimes whenever viable opportunities are encountered

**normative validation:** an effect of punishing wrongdoing whereby people's perception of the behavior as deviant is reinforced

**objective punishment properties:** likelihood that certain punishments will reduce criminal behavior

**panopticon:** a prison design developed by Jeremy Bentham to allow observation down all wings of cells from a central location

**perceptions of punishment:** likelihood of a person realizing that he or she will be punished for committing a crime; knowledge of certainty and severity of punishment

**positive criminology:** the school of thought that views crime as a product of forces beyond the rational control of individuals and is based on the scientific method

**preclassical criminology:** era when the social context for classical criminology emerged

**quartering:** a medieval torture in which persons were put to death by attaching horses to all four limbs and severing them from the body by driving the horses in different directions

**rational choice:** the ability to think about something in a rational, calculating fashion while weighing the costs and benefits of that action

**restrictive deterrence:** the prevention of some, but not all, crime through threats of sanctions; also called *marginal deterrence*

**retribution:** "deserts serving"; something given in recompense

**routine activities theory:** proposed by Lawrence Cohen and Marcus Felson to explain rising crime in the 1970s; a theory of victimization; comprised of three variables that contributed to the likelihood of the crime being committed

**shaming:** an informal control of crime or deviance where society reacts to undesired behavior in order to deter that behavior

**specific deterrence:** sanctions intended to prevent additional offenses by the punished offender; the concept is to teach them a lesson

**suitable targets:** something of value that is available to a potential offender

**target hardening:** taking steps to minimize the likelihood that you will be the victim of a crime

**tiger prevention fallacy:** a humorous analogy drawn to illustrate the widespread fallacy that absence of crime demonstrates the effectiveness of deterrence efforts; the story identifies a man snapping his fingers in the middle of New York City and claiming that his efforts have deterred tigers from congregating

**tipping levels:** the idea that punishment certainty, severity, and celerity must reach a minimum level before a deterrent effect can be realized

**utilitarianism:** the philosophical position that actions should be judged by their usefulness; referred to by Bentham as the "greatest happiness principle"

**victimology:** the study of why people are victimized and how the routine activities/lifestyle of a person can affect their risk of victimization

**warden's survey:** a humorous analogy drawn to illustrate the widespread fallacy that the presence of crime demonstrates that deterrence does not work; the story identifies a prison warden pointing to his inmates as proof of the absence of deterrence

## Key Criminologists

**Cesare Beccaria:** author of *On Crimes and Punishment* (1864) and credited as the leading organizer of classical thinking on criminology and deterrence theory

**Jeremy Bentham:** an English utilitarian philosopher and reformer who contributed much to classical thinking in the late eighteenth and early nineteenth century

**Lawrence Cohen:** came up with the routine activities theory, a theory of victimization, with Marcus Felson to explain rising crime rates in the 1970s

**Marcus Felson:** came up with the routine activities theory, a theory of victimization, with Lawrence Cohen to explain rising crime rates in the 1970s

**Robert Martinson:** a researcher whose works in the 1970s contributed to emergence of the "anti-rehabilitation" movement and popularized the phrase regarding correction treatment that "nothing works"

**Raymond Paternoster:** a criminologist who has made significant contributions to the perceptual deterrence literature

**Sir Robert Peel:** the Home Secretary of England responsible for passage of the London Metropolitan Police Act in 1829; this introduced the first modern policing system and was based on the principles of deterrence

**Alex Piquero:** with Raymond Paternoster, found that perceived certainty of arrest was associated with reporting of less drinking and driving

**Greg Pogarsky:** developed a tripartite conceptual schema of deterrability; at one end of the continuum are the incorrigible and at the other end are the acute conformists

**Sir Samuel Romilly:** a member of the English House of Commons in the early nineteenth century who was a staunch advocate of classical humanitarian reforms

**Charles Tittle:** criminologist whose research contributed to empirical and conceptual clarity in the early phases of contemporary deterrence research; conducted extensive research and testing of the differential association model proposed by Edwin Sutherland; his research has focused on the deficiencies in the causal framework set out by Sutherland; a chief opponent of labeling theory; Tittle claims that propositions of the labeling perspective are not clearly identified so as to allow for empirical research and believes the theory to be too vague

Chapter 6
# Biogenic and Psychogenic Theories of Crime

---

## Summary

The positive school, focusing on biological and psychogenic factors as potential causes of crime, was strongly influenced by scientific developments in the late nineteenth century, such as Charles Darwin's work regarding evolution. Positivism views crime as being caused by factors beyond the control of individuals. It focuses on criminals rather than crimes, seeking to determine the factors that cause individuals to commit crime and then control these factors by scientific methods. Modern criminologists adopting a positivistic view state that certain factors increase the likelihood of criminality rather than declaring that individuals possessing those characteristics will be criminal. Some positive criminologists oppose biogenic and psychogenic criminological theories, insisting instead that social factors cause crime. Across time, however, the biological and psychological ideas of crime have become more accepted. Different theories have become widely accepted and continue to grow today.

## Criminal Anthropology

An early concept in biological and psychological positivism was criminal anthropology, which assumed that criminals were abnormal. Cesare Lombroso, an Italian physician, thought at first that all criminals were atavists, or throwbacks to an earlier stage of evolution. Lombroso considered these individuals "born criminals," who could be identified by physical characteristics. As Lombroso conducted further research, he reduced his estimate of atavists in the criminal population to around one-third. He labeled the rest "ciminaloids," or minor offenders. Lombroso, along with his son-in-law, William Ferrero, was one of the first researchers to study the criminality of females, though his work was plagued by flaws.

Enrico Ferri rejected the search for a single explanation of crime causation in favor of a multiple factor approach. Ferri favored assigning different punishments to different offenders who committed similar crimes, with the punishments based on the characteristics of the offenders rather than on the seriousness of the crimes.

Raffaele Garofalo preferred a sociological definition of crime to a legal one. He thought society should dispose of criminals, modeling Darwin's thesis of survival of the fittest.

Charles Goring favored criminal anthropology, but criticized Lombroso for failing to use instruments to make his measurements. Goring's work undermined many of Lombroso's ideas, but he determined that body types were correlated with certain types of crimes.

Harvard University physical anthropologist Earnest A. Hooten described criminals as organically inferior and believed that crime could only be understood through biology. He also believed that society should eliminate criminal offenders, and he tried to substantiate Lombroso's findings, but his work also suffered from methodological flaws.

William Sheldon developed a biological approach called *constitutional psychology,* based on body types. Endomorphs were described as soft and round; mesomorphs were muscular; and ectomorphs were lean. According to Sheldon, delinquents were high in mesomorphy and low in ectomorphy.

## Criminal Heredity

Family studies, such as Henry Goddard's study of the Kallikaks, have shown that good hereditary factors combined with good homes are likely to result in solid citizens. However, such studies have failed to distinguish between the effects of heredity and the effects of environment. These efforts that have been made to link genetic traits to criminal behavior by studying families in which criminal activity was widespread through generations are termed *eugenics*.

## Contemporary Biological Perspectives

Twin studies have been carried out mostly in Scandinavian countries such as Denmark because they maintain records on twins and police contacts that make data readily available. Researchers examining the criminal records of twins look for concordance, which is the percentage of cases in which both twins have been identified as criminal offenders or non-offenders. If identical twins, who share their entire genetic makeup, show a greater incidence of criminal concordance than other types of siblings, this would support the hypothesis that heritable factors contribute to criminal behavior. Such studies typically have revealed a higher rate of concordance among identical twins than among fraternal twins and non-twin siblings, but environment may still be having an effect. In further support of a genetic criminal trait, adoption studies, such as that by Barry Hutchings and Sarnoff Mednick, have indicated that adopted children are more likely to offend if their biological fathers have criminal records than if their adopted fathers have criminal records.

Levels of the male hormone testosterone are inheritable, and elevated testosterone levels have been linked to deviance. Premenstrual syndrome (PMS) has provided a successful defense to criminal charges in France. Recent evidence has also begun to show support for the importance of diet as a variable to help explain behavior, including deviant and criminal acts. Other biological factors that have been connected with criminality or violence include hypoglycemia, sugar intake, and low levels of neurotransmitters, such as serotonin. Environmental neurotoxins like nicotine and lead may also play a role.

Several studies have examined the possible link of genetic traits to criminal behavior through eugenics. Some popular historical studies include Henry Goddard's study of *The Kallikak Family* and Richard Dugdale's *The Jukes: A Study in Crime, Pauperism, Disease and Heredity* (1877). Today, biological explanations appear to be gaining credibility once again. In addition to becoming more multidisciplinary, biologically inclusive criminology is beginning to look more at nature *and* nurture, instead of nature vs. nurture. Biological theories are now seeing outcomes as a sum of biological *risk factors*, combined with a wide range of environmental influences.

Another theoretical perspective that sees functioning of the brain as central to understanding deviant patterns of behavior posits variation in the level of stimulation necessary for arousal of the cerebral cortex. *Arousal theory* asserts that those with low arousal of the brain require a lot of neurological stimulation to achieve a feeling of emotional balance. These individuals seek out stimulation through exciting activities, which may include criminal behaviors.

*Sociobiology*, or *evolutionary psychology*, asserts that humans continuously evolve and the natural survival instinct of males to reproduce has facilitated the evolution of male "cheaters."

## Psychogenic Theories of Crime

Psychogenic theories have been under stack for years from criminologists who place higher value on social theory and political ideology. If psychology is the study of the mind, then criminal psychology is the study of the criminal mind. Many psychologists will incorporate biological variables in understanding the function of the mind, and thus it becomes difficult to distinguish between psychological and biological explanations of crime. There are also differences between psychiatry and psychology. Sigmund Freud founded the Freudian psychoanalytic perspective. He argues that unconscious forces drive the human personality, and many of those forces are related to sexual desires. This personality contains three separate components: the id, ego, and superego.

Hans Eysenck developed the Eysenckian theory. His *conditioning theory* asserts that criminals have personalities that differ from those of noncriminals. Eysenck argued that mainstream criminological theories that emphasized social variables held little value when explaining crime. At the root of his theory are two major shaping forces: one's inherited nervous system, and environmental conditioning forces. These forces impact three critical features of the personality: extraversion, neuroticism, and psychoticism.

## Psychogenic Factors in Criminal Behavior

Psychological theories assume that something within individuals causes criminal behavior. Scales on both the Minnesota Multiphasic Personality Inventory (MMPI) and the California Personality Inventory (CPI) have been shown to be correlated with criminal behavior. People with antisocial personalities, once referred to as *psychopaths*, experience little or no guilt and are motivated by self-gratification. Crimes committed by such persons rarely are thought to be planned in advance.

## Key Terms

**antisocial personality:** persons who once were labeled psychopaths; characterized by high impulsivity, an inability to form lasting relationships with others, and the trait of experiencing little or no guilt when inflicting harm

**arousal (cortical):** neurological simulation

**arousal theory:** asserts that those with low arousal levels require greater levels of stimulation and seek exciting activities, which may include criminal activities, to achieve emotional balance

**atavism:** possessing qualities of more primitive ancestors; Lombroso classified such biological throwbacks as "born criminals"

**behavioral genetics:** an approach that looks at the contribution of genetics and environment to any given phenotype

**bipolar disorder:** manic depression

**born criminal:** a person destined by his or her degenerate state to commit criminal acts, as Lombroso's description of atavists

**community corrections:** the idea that offenders will be more responsive to treatment within a community

**concordance:** in twin studies, the percentage of cases in which both twins are identified as offenders or non-offenders

**conditioning theory:** theory that asserts that criminals have personalities different from those of noncriminals

**constitutional psychology:** biological approach developed by William Sheldon; body types influence behavior

**criminal anthropology:** the biological, psychological, and sociological study of criminal offenders

**criminaloids:** minor offenders

**determinism:** an assumption of positivism that says that individual differences are rooted in factors beyond, or at least not entirely within, the control of individuals

**ectomorph:** one of three somatotypes, or bodily forms, described as lean; Sheldon found delinquents to be low in ectomorphy

**ego:** according to Freud, is the mediating force, often called the conscious personality

**empiricism:** the idea that knowledge must be obtained through observation and experimentation

**endomorph ego:** type of temperament characterized by need for company, affection, and social support; do not tend to be delinquent types

**environmental neurotoxins:** biological variables such as nicotine and lead

**eugenics:** approach that links genetic traits to criminal behavior

**evolutionary psychology:** also known as sociobiology; asserts that humans continuously evolve

**extravert:** personality characterized by outgoing, risk-taking, and impulsive behavior

**feebleminded:** label for person functioning below the normal intellectual range but above the level designated "idiot"

**genotype:** the genetic makeup of an individual

**id:** consists of drives that underlie all human behavior

**indeterminate sentence:** open-ended sentence; calls for release of offender after the offender has been cured or rehabilitated

**introvert:** this individual requires very low levels of stimulation; opposite of the extravert

**Jukes:** family study done by Richard Dugdale; showed link between genetics and criminal behavior

**Kallikak family:** family study done by Henry Goddard; showed the significance of heredity as it relates to behavior

**libido:** the sex drive

**Medical Model:** positivism calls for a medicalization of criminality and thus becomes known as the medical model

**mesomorph:** one of three somatotypes, or bodily forms, described as muscular; Sheldon found delinquents to be high in mesomorphy

**MMPI:** Minnesota Multiphasic Personality Inventory, a 556-item test consisting of 10 clinical scales; are said to show a relationship between measures of psychopathic deviancy, schizophrenia, and hypomania (unproductive hyperactivity) and later delinquency

**nature vs. nurture:** debate over whether biological or social factors have the larger influence over behavior

**neuroticism:** refers to someone's degree of emotionality

**neurotransmitters:** chemical messengers in the brain that allow neural cells to communicate with each other

**non-shared environmental influences:** environmental interactions specific to an individual

**Paradigm Revolution:** first natural explanation of crime; a dramatic shift in the theoretical orientation and underlying assumptions for explaining a phenomenon

**phrenology:** school of thought that associated criminality with abnormalities in the brain

**PMS:** premenstrual syndrome; may be characterized by physical and psychological symptoms that spark violent acts in some women

**polymorphisms:** many patterns of imbalanced genetic structures

**positivism:** criminological school stipulating that human behavior is determined by factors beyond, or at least not entirely within the control of, the actor and insisting that criminologists must employ the scientific methods of the physical sciences to identify these causal forces

**probation:** identification of some offenders eligible for community-based treatment instead of incarceration

**projection:** according to Freud, this occurs when a person with repressed drives believes that many other people possess these drives

**psychopath:** person who is now referred to as having an antisocial personality, characterized by high impulsivity, an inability to form lasting relationships with others, and the trait of experiencing little or no guilt when inflicting harm

**reaction formation:** the exaggeration of someone's behavior to the opposite extreme of sexual desire; according to Freud, instead of reacting to sexual desires, this person may declare celibacy

**repression:** according to Freud, this will occur when someone denies that his or her sexual desires exist

**risk factors:** variables that may increase or decrease an individual's chances of becoming criminal

**schizophrenia:** characterized by a person's having dramatic misperceptions of the world and inappropriate emotions; is rooted in neurobiology

**serotonin:** a neurotransmitter, or chemical messenger in the brain that allows neural cells to communicate with one another

**shared environmental influences:** common social experiences within a family

**sociobiology:** also known as evolutionary psychology; contends that humans continuously evolve

**somatotypes:** distinctive bodily forms thought to influence behavior; the types were labeled endomorph (soft and round), mesomorph (muscular), and ectomorph (lean)

**statistical school:** preceded Lombroso with the initiation of the scientific study of crime by nearly half a century; the statistical school is socially oriented

**sublimation:** channeling drives into socially approved activities

**superego:** the conscience; represents moral standards of society

**testosterone:** male sex hormone; frequently studied with regard toward criminal violence

## Key Criminologists

**Karl O. Christiansen:** studied the records of 3,586 twins born between 1881 and 1910 in Denmark, finding the highest rates of criminal concordance among identical twins; Christiansen acknowledged the possibility of some environmental effect on this finding

**Charles Darwin:** author of *On the Origin of Species* and *The Descent of Man*; believed that science could offer answers to questions concerning human problems

**Richard Dugdale:** studied the family history of a fictitiously named family, the Jukes; study showed a link between heredity and criminal behavior

**Lee Ellis:** studied arrest records of juveniles; discovered that approximately 40 percent of juvenile males in the United States had been arrested; also did studies on cheater theory

**Arthur H. Estabrook:** eugenicist who revised and expanded Dugan's study of the Jukes; published *The Jukes* in 1915

**Hans Eysenck:** psychobiologist who spent years developing a theory of crime that asserts that criminals have personalities that differ from those of noncriminals; Eysenck placed emphasis on the heritability of neurological predisposition for criminality

**William Ferrero:** along with his father-in-law, Cesare Lombroso, was a pioneer in the study of crime committed by women

**Enrico Ferri:** Italian criminologist of the late eighteenth century and colleague of Lombroso who developed positivism into a multiple factor approach, seeking many different causes for a single criminal act; he strongly opposed the classical tradition and argued that punishments should be tailored to the background and traits of the offenders

**Diana H. Fishbein:** although agreeing that twin studies offer some evidence that genetic make-up affects behavior, she argues that genetic influences need to be studied more rigorously

**Sigmund Freud:** associated with traditional psychiatry; founded the Freudian psychoanalytic perspective, which is the assumption that the human personality is driven by unconscious forces, many of them related to sexual desires

**Raffaele Garofalo:** Italian criminologist of the early twentieth century who rejected the legal definition of crime for a sociological approach; believed in ridding society of criminal offenders by execution or exile

**Eleanor and Sheldon Glueck:** well-known criminologists in the mid-twentieth century who matched 500 delinquents and nondelinquents, finding that delinquents were considerably more mesomorphic than nondelinquents and their ranks contained a much lower proportion of ectomorphs

**Henry Goddard:** wrote *The Kallikak Family* (1912/1955), in which he traced two lineages of Martin Kallikak, one legitimate, the other illegitimate; his argument was that this supported genetic determination, but he failed to control for environmental factors

**Charles Goring:** medical officer in the English prisons and author of *The English Convict* (1913), in which he highlighted biological determinism but criticized Lombroso for relying on observations rather than instruments for measurement

**A.M. Guery:** French social statistician; first to analyze geographic-based data in a search of a relationship between crime and social characteristics

**Earnest Hooton:** Harvard University physical anthropologist who proclaimed criminals to be organically inferior and suggested they be eliminated or completely segregated from society

**John Laub:** along with Robert Sampson, insisted that Sutherland and the sociologists intended to turn the study of crime into an exclusively sociological enterprise (a revisionist view)

**Cesare Lombroso:** nineteenth-century Italian physician who adopted a social Darwinian perspective, maintaining that humans demonstrate different levels of biological development; Lombroso developed the concept of atavism; although none of Lombroso's specific theories are accepted today, he was the first person to apply scientific principles to the study of criminals

**Henry Mayhew:** Englishman who took a sociological approach in analyzing official data and detailed observations; best known representative of statistical school

**Terrie Moffitt:** psychogenic researcher who argues deficiencies, such as neuropsychological deficits, can be associated with law-abiding behavior as well as crime, depending upon the life circumstances of the individual

**Adolphe Quetelet:** known as the "father of modern statistics"; refuted the notion of free will and sought propensities for crime through the analysis of social data

**Robert Sampson:** along with John Laub, insisted that Sutherland and the sociologists intended to turn the study of crime into an exclusively sociological enterprise (a revisionist view)

**William Sheldon:** introduced the concept of constitutional psychology; found delinquents to be decidedly high in mesomorphy and low in ectomorphy

**Edwin Sutherland:** sociologist who elevated criminology to a respectable status within that discipline; disassociated criminology from biology, psychology, and other disciplines

# Chapter 7
# Social Structure Theories of Crime

## Summary

Social structure theorists envision criminal behavior as the product of social forces and focus on the structural deficiencies that can attribute to the increased probability that individuals will engage in criminal behavior. Although the social structure theories are macro-level theories, there have been arguments by some criminologists that defend the idea that these theories adequately explain individual-level crime because the individual mirrors the group. The social structure theories are based upon three underlying assumptions. First, these theories argue that the structure in which society is built is in some way deficient. Second, these types of theories focus on crime as a lower-class phenomenon. Third, the social structure theories are macro-level theories intended to explain rates of crime among groups, not individual-level offending. They are concerned with identifying the structural factors that increase the odds that an individual will engage in deviant behavior. Two main subtheories of the social structure theory include the strain theories and the social ecological theories.

## Strain Theory

This particular branch of the social structure theory argues that stress, frustration, and strain increase the likelihood that an individual will engage in delinquent behavior. Norm violation occurs as a result of trying to alleviate the stress and strain placed on the individual. Many strain theorists recognize that the greatest amount of strain is evident in the lower-class groups.

Emile Durkheim was a French sociologist who believed that individual behavior was shaped by larger social phenomena. He looked extensively at the dynamics of suicide. In his book *Suicide* (1897), Durkheim identifies four categories of suicides. Durkheim hypothesized that anomie contributes to suicide. The concept of anomie, or a state of normlessness, became the basis for later strain theories.

Robert Merton took the concept of anomie and developed his own strain theory in *Social Structure and Anomie* (1938). Merton asserts that society is delineating which goals are desirable and which means are acceptable forms in which to achieve those goals. Merton identified the main prominent goal of American society as the acquisition of wealth. Society emphasizes wealth without providing equal access to the legitimate means by which to obtain it. This is the source for anomie and strain. As a result of this strain, those individuals who do not have access to either the legitimate goals or the legitimate means begin to engage in behavior deemed deviant in order to alleviate the strain. The means by which an individual copes is outlined in Merton's individual modes of adaptation. The five categories are conformity, innovation, ritualism, retreatism, and rebellion.

Twenty years later, Richard Cloward and Lloyd Ohlin expanded upon Merton's theory. They were developing a model that would explain juvenile gang delinquency based upon the innovator category of Merton's modes of adaptation. The opportunity theory, as their version of strain was called, claimed that the different types of illegitimate opportunity structures available to the juveniles influenced the type of delinquent activities in which they became involved. They identified three types of gangs: criminal, conflict, and retreatist. Depending on the opportunities available and the organization of the individuals' neighborhoods, the delinquents could become involved in any of these three categories.

Criminologist Robert Agnew addressed the criticisms with the earlier strain theorists and proposed a general strain theory. Agnew identifies three types of strain-inducing stimuli: first, failure to achieve goals; second, removal of positively valued stimuli; third, the presence of negatively valued stimuli. Virtually everyone experiences one or more of these types of strains, but it is the individual's interpretation of the source of strain that is the determining factor of whether illegal activity will occur. Research has found that the general strain theory did a moderately good job of explaining delinquency and drug use.

Rekindling the macro-level perspective of strain offered by Merton, 50 years later Steven Messner and Richard Rosenfeld proposed that it was the American dream that is the root cause of the high volume of crime.

## Assessing Strain Theories

The biggest criticism that the strain theorists receive refers to its assumption that crime is a lower-class problem. Some theorists argue that it appears to be a phenomenon present only in the lower class due to bias reporting and discrimination within the system. Others offer the notion that persons of other classes may too experience strain due to other social structure features. The biggest criticism comes from the ambiguity of operationalizing the variables. Concepts such as aspirations and hopes are very abstract and hard to measure.

The strain theories had significant impact on the policies implemented during the administrations of both John F. Kennedy and Lyndon B. Johnson. Programs were designed to alleviate poverty and enhance opportunities. Ideas put forth by Cohen seem to indicate that the environment of the public school system needs to be adjusted to accommodate lower-class youths and minimize their frustrations.

## Social Ecology

This perspective focuses on the person's relation to the social environment and owes its conceptualization to the research conducted by members of the Chicago School. The early researchers identified "natural areas" of the cities. The concentric zone model claims that these natural areas of the city expand radially from a central business area. Robert Park identified five different zones of the concentric zone model.

Using the model of concentric zones developed by Robert Park, Clifford Shaw and Henry McKay studied the rates of crime in each zone to find out if there was a relation to the social condition of the zone. Indeed, Shaw and McKay were able to identify specific characteristics that were present in areas with high delinquency rates. The zone of transition had the highest rate of criminal activity and was plagued by many of the factors that lead to social disorganization. The Chicago Area Project was implemented to help improve the conditions of the communities where crime rates were very high in hopes of being able to prevent the cultural transmission of delinquency. This project later became the basis for community prevention programs implemented during the 1960s.

## Contemporary Social Ecology

Contemporary research of the social ecology/social disorganization perspectives are beginning to utilize new techniques such as self-report and victimization data. The expanded use of factor-analysis is being used so that researchers can better examine trends over time. One major criticism of the social ecological theories centers around their inability to prevent the occurrence of ecological fallacy. W.S. Robinson has been a staunch opponent of this perspective due to the significant inferential error that seems to exist in social ecological studies.

## Key Terms

**altruistic suicide:** category of suicide described by Emile Durkheim where the individual is deeply committed to the norms of a group and as an expression of loyalty takes his or her own life

**anomie:** concept introduced by Emile Durkheim that refers to a state of normlessness; a condition in society in which norms are no longer effective in regulating behavior

**Chicago Area Project:** conducted in three high-delinquency areas from 1932 to 1957; the basic idea was to organize local residents of these areas to help improve the community in hoes of reducing crime

**Chicago School:** refers to research being conducted at the University of Chicago department of sociology during the 1920s through the 1940s; its members assisted in moving research findings on crime from strictly laboratory findings to actual testing of such findings in the field

**concentric zone model:** identified in the research done by Park and Burgess, members of the Chicago School; this model identified five zones growing radially from the central business district, each having distinct social characteristics

**conflict gang:** according to Cloward and Ohlin's opportunity theory, this group has blocked legitimate means of achieving goals and, as well, due to social disorganization of the neighborhood, probably has blocked illegitimate opportunity structures; this group turns to destructive and violent behavior, usually emphasizing physical prowess as an important value

**conformity:** accepting both culturally specified goals and abiding by culturally approved means for pursuit of those goals

**criminal gang:** a vehicle for pursuit of illegitimate goals available in communities well-organized enough to provide the necessary structure

**cultural transmission:** the idea that a tradition of delinquent behavior is handed down from one generation to the next due to an absence of community values

**ecological fallacy:** occurs when correlations obtained at the macro-theory level are substituted for individual-level correlations; additionally, this can also occur when findings are generalized from one part of the country to another, not taking cultural differences into account

**goals and means:** described by Robert Merton in his version of anomie theory; goals are the socially approved values; means refers to the acceptable methods in which to achieve these goals

**innovation:** this type of offender subscribes to the same social goals as mainstream society, but his or her opportunities to achieve such goals by conventional methods are blocked; the innovator then turns to methods that may be viewed as socially unacceptable, but nonetheless allows for him or her to achieve the same goals as conventional society

**institutional anomie theory:** theory that social institutions place pressure upon people differentially throughout the class structure; society denotes socially approved values and goals that exert pressure on people

**myth of classlessness:** the strain theories are based upon the implicit assumption that there is a direct relationship between low-class and criminal behavior; critics argue that in fact this is merely a "myth" and the only reason it appears to be so is because of the bias in official statistics

**opportunity theory:** developed by Cloward and Ohlin, who expanded on Robert Merton's strain theory; this theory looks to explaining gang delinquency and the different opportunity structures available to them; Cloward and Ohlin argue that in addition to legitimate means, illegitimate opportunity structures must exist and be available before criminality will occur

**reaction formation:** introduced by Albert Cohen, this concept refers to the exaggerated efforts to deny and reject that which is actually desired

**rebellion:** category of Merton's modes of adaptation that is made up of those who have rejected the goals and means of conventional society and supplanted them with a whole new set of values and norms

**retreatism:** category of Merton's modes of adaptation that is made up of those who have dropped out of society; they have rejected both the means and the goals of mainstream society and are completely unconcerned with implanting new ones

**retreatist gang:** the delinquent subculture identified in opportunity theory that is composed of the social dropouts, the double losers; this group does not have the access to illegitimate opportunities nor do they have what it takes to become part of the conflict gang

**ritualism:** category of Merton's modes of adaptation that is made up of those who have abandoned the goals of society but still subscribe to the conventional means by which to achieve those goals

**social disorganization:** identified by Cloward and Ohlin as an important component contributing to the blocked access to illegitimate opportunity structures; areas with high social disorganization, characterized by poverty, residential mobility, and racial heterogeneity are less likely to have access to illegitimate opportunity structures

**social ecology:** the study of the relation of the organism to its environment; within criminology, this branch focuses on an individual and how that individual relates to the social environment

**social organization:** identified by Cloward and Ohlin as an important component contributing to access to illegitimate opportunity structures; areas with good social organization are more likely to have access to illegitimate opportunity structures

**social structure theories:** macro-theories that assume that crime is primarily a lower-class problem due to social factors that contribute to poverty, unemployment, and poor education; they look to flaws within the social structure of society that increases the odds that an individual will engage in illegal behavior

**sociobiology:** a combination of sociological and biological explanations of crime; illustrative of the current trend to integrate theories in an attempt to better explain crime and criminal behavior

**strain theories:** based upon the assumption that due to the structure of society, pressure is being exerted on individuals in the lower class, causing strain; in order to alleviate or relieve the strain, these individuals are engaging in behavior that is contrary to the values and norms of conventional society

## Key Criminologists

**Robert Agnew:** developed a general strain theory in the 1990s to expand the theory beyond the scope of explaining lower-class street crime

**Robert J. Bursik, Jr.:** along with Janet Heitgard, examined the effects of neighborhood racial change and other indicators of social disorganization upon delinquency rates in adjoining areas; found that delinquency rates increased as a consequence of rapid compositional changes in adjoining neighborhoods

**Richard Cloward:** along with Lloyd Ohlin, expanded upon the work of Robert Merton and looked specifically at juvenile gang delinquency; they developed the opportunity theory, which focuses on the illegitimate opportunity structures available to the juvenile gangs

**Emile Durkheim:** French sociologist who developed the concept of anomie through his research on suicide; anomie has become the foundation on which the strain theories are built

**Henry McKay:** prominent criminologist who expanded on the works of the Chicago School to develop the social ecological theory of crime; research of the concentric zones of the city helped to identify some aggravating conditions that may account for higher levels of criminal behavior

**Robert Merton:** renowned criminologist whose article "Social Structure and Anomie" (1938) became one of the most influential pieces of strain theory literature; he focuses on goals and means of society and argues that blocked means by which to achieve the goals is the cause of strain; this strain in turn leads to anomie; he identified five individual modes of adaptation to this anomie

**Steven Messner:** along with Richard Rosenfeld, proposed that it was the American dream that is the root cause of the high volume of crime

**Lloyd Ohlin:** along with Richard Cloward, developed the opportunity theory, which expanded upon Robert Merton's theory of anomie

**Richard Rosenfeld:** along with Steven Messner, proposed that it was the American dream that is the root cause of the high volume of crime

**Clifford Shaw:** social ecological theorist responsible for developing the social ecological theory; along with Henry McKay expanded on earlier research done by the Chicago School on ecological explanations of criminal activity

**Edwin Sutherland:** did extensive research on white-collar crime wherein he coined the term "white-collar crime"; he developed the differential association theory, which believes deviance is a learned behavior taken from significant others; he argues that in addition to the importance of learning the techniques necessary to commit crime, an individual must also learn the value system that accompanies them so that engaging in deviant behavior is possible

Chapter 8
# Social Process Theories of Crime

## Summary

Social process theories represent a shift from macro theory to micro theory. They focus more on the explanations for individual law violations. They differ from the social structure theory in that they do not view crime as being predominantly a lower-class problem. Through the use of self-report surveys, researchers are finding that crime and delinquency seem to be more equally distributed among all classes than was previously thought.

Learning, culture conflict, and social control theories are all considered to be a part of the social process perspective. All three types of theories share the assumption that groups influence the individual. The common goal for each type of theory is to account for crime across all social classes.

## Learning Criminal Behavior

The first type of social process theory is referred to as the learning perspective. The learning theorist believes that deviant behavior is learned in a social context. An underlying assumption of the learning theory is crime is "normal" rather than "pathological" due to the process by which one learns deviant behavior.

## Edwin H. Sutherland—Differential Association

Differential association can be regarded as one of the most prominent theories of criminal behavior. Sutherland displaced the biological and psychological explanations of the earlier twentieth century with a more sociological based theory that was intended to explain all crime. In addition to its significance in the criminal justice field, Sutherland also succeeded in bringing the field of criminology under the sociological umbrella.

Influences such as symbolic interactionism, introduced by George Mead; cultural transmission, developed by the Chicago School; and culture conflict, first introduced by Thorsten Sellin assisted in Sutherland's development of differential association theory. Sutherland was particularly interested in the area of white-collar crime and, in fact, actually coined the term *white-collar crime* in his book of the same name published in 1949.

Differential association theory is based upon nine principles that identify the process by which a person comes to engage in crime. At the base of this theory is the belief that deviant behavior is a learned behavior. Sutherland believed this behavior to be learned within intimate personal groups. He recognizes that there must be a process by which an individual can learn the specific techniques necessary to carry out the deviant act and, in addition, the person must also be taught the value system that accompanies such behavior. Criminal behavior will occur when an individual's definitions favorable for committing crime outweigh the unfavorable.

## Criticisms of Differential Association

The main criticism comes from the inability to adequately test and verify the theory through empirical research. Consistency in the operationalization of the variables has also been very difficult to achieve due to the vagueness and abstractness of concepts such as excess, definitions, and association. The differential association theory has also been criticized for being entirely too broad and thus is ineffective in explaining any crime.

## Ronald Akers—Social Learning Theory

Ron Akers expanded Sutherland's differential association by adding components of operant and respondent conditioning. Akers assumed that criminal behavior did not differ from conforming behavior and that both theories could be explained by social learning theory. The basic idea of the social learning theory is that criminal behavior occurs as a result of deviant behavior being differentially reinforced and defined as desirable. He identified four key elements that help shape behavior: differential associations, definitions, differential reinforcement, and imitation.

## Tests of Social Learning Theory

The two main criticisms of the social learning approach are that the theory is tautological in nature, and the temporal sequencing of peer association and delinquency is poorly specified. Current research seems to support the social learning hypothesis in terms of the temporal sequencing issue. The social learning theory has received consistent empirical support and has fared well in explaining partner and family violence.

## Culture Conflict and Crime

The basis of this approach comes from the belief that the conflict of values of different cultures or subcultures can cause criminal or delinquent behavior. Subculture theories assume that crime is a lower-class problem. They also see deviance as normal rather than pathological due to its being part of the learning process that is part of the subcultural code.

## Thorsten Sellin—Conflict of Conduct Norms

Thorsten Sellin began to move criminology away from a legalistic definition of crime to more of a normative definition. He became interested in the field of criminology, developing laws of human nature, and more specifically explaining violations of conduct norms. The culture conflict theory developed by Sellin argues that sometimes the norms of conventional society may clash with the norms of the subculture, and no matter how an individual acts, there will be violation of norms for one of the two groups. Crime, then, can be explained in terms of norms learned in a subculture that are not represented in the legal codes.

## Marvin Wolfgang and Franco Ferracuti— Subculture of Violence

Interested in explaining homicides and assaults that occur spontaneously, Wolfgang and Ferracuti conducted extensive research that yielded the development of the subculture of violence theory. They found that most violence occurred in the heat of passion as opposed to being premeditated or psychotic. They also discovered that most spontaneous violence was prevalent among late teens to middle-aged males in lower-class settings. Wolfgang and Ferracuti do not see the subculture as being distinctly separate from the larger culture, but rather the subculture is founded on a "notion of honor." Violent or physically aggressive responses are either expected or required in order to defend "honor."

Empirical test of the subculture of violence theory have yielded mixed results. Some theorists might argue that the violent subculture identified by Wolfgang and Ferracuti may be attributed to the social structure of society rather than due to a unique value system upon which the subculture may be based.

## Elijah Anderson—Code of the Street

Anderson took an approach to explain the disproportional amount of violence seen in young African American males. Similar to Wolfgang and Ferracuti's "notion of honor," Anderson used the "code of the street" to explain this violence. This street code is adopted as a response to structural problems and leads to a cycle of violence.

## Walter Miller—Lower-Class Focal Concerns

This perspective is grounded in learning theory and ecological data. Walter Miller observed lower-class male gang members in their natural habitat over the course of three years and concluded that these lower-class individuals had developed a value system separate from mainstream American society. He identified these values as being the six focal concerns. According to Miller, trouble, toughness, smartness, excitement, fate, and autonomy were the most important values of the subculture that he observed.

## Analysis of Focal Concerns

Miller offers a contrast to the strain theories that assume that strain comes from the inability of lower-class individuals to achieve the same goals as the middle- and upper-class individuals. Miller disagrees and states that there really is no strain because the people of the lower class or of the subcultures really do not have the same goals as middle- and upper-class persons. A major criticism of Miller's theory is that it only addressed male delinquency. Some have found the theory to be tautological in nature.

## Social Control and Crime

These types of theories represent a sharp contrast to the other social process theories. The social control theories have a dimmer view of human nature and assert that if an individual was left alone, he or she would pursue self-interests rather than what is good for society. The control theorists think that conformity comes from imposing a controlled social existence.

## Gresham M. Sykes and David Matza—Techniques of Neutralization

Sykes and Matza were interested in the learned excuses that may be situationally invoked to allow boys to engage in behavior that was not in accordance with their normal value system. They became interested in the phenomenon they later developed into the drift theory that allows for an individual to engage in episodic bouts of criminality while still upholding their larger values. The techniques of neutralization allowed for an individual to engage in behavior that would normally violate the norms and still preserve the self-image of a norm follower. Neutralization must precede the offense, whereas rationalization occurs following the norm-violating behavior. The five techniques are denial of responsibility, denial of injury, denial of victim, condemnation of the condemners, and appeal to higher loyalties.

## Analysis of Neutralization

Research and empirical support for neutralization theory is very slight. In spite of weak empirical support, neutralization theory has had tremendous impact on the development of the social control perspective. Recent research has shown that neutralization might particularly apply to white-collar crimes.

## Travis Hirschi—Social Bond Theory

Travis Hirschi's contention that a person becomes delinquent when his or her ties to conventional society have been broken is the premise upon which his social bonding theory was developed. He maintains a very negative view of human nature and seeks to find out why the individuals in society do not violate the law, rather than why criminals do violate the law. The social bonding theory presupposes normative consensus and believes that increasing the "stakes in conformity" would lead to a decrease in deviant behavior. Hirschi identified four components of the social bonding process: attachment, commitment, involvement, and belief. Attachment has by far been accorded the most attention, with attachments to family and school being the best predictors of conformity.

## Analysis of Social Bond

Social bonding theory was one of the few theories that was subjected to substantial empirical testing during its developmental stages. One chief criticism of the theory is that it excluded a whole population of subjects: females. In fact, Hirschi's theory was based upon research conducted only on young males. Since its origin, some criminologists have tested the concepts of the social bonding theory on females and have found it to have a strong explanatory power. Causal order appears to be an area of deficiency. Almost all the tests of the social bonding theory have been cross-sectional, thus failing to address causal order. Longitudinal research conducted by Robert Agnew found weak support, raising questions as to its explanatory power.

## Michael Gottfredson and Travis Hirschi— A General Theory of Crime

This ambitious theory maintains that all criminal and analogous behavior can be explained by low self-control. The origins of self-control lie in early childhood socialization. It is fixed by age eight and remains constant across life (a concept that has recently come under increasing criticism). Some argue that the theory is tautological. It has not yet been subjected to a wide range of empirical testing.

## Key Terms

**analogous acts:** deviant and risky behaviors thought by some criminologists to be products of the same causal forces as crimes

**appeal to higher loyalties:** element of Sykes and Matza's neutralization theory wherein neutralization occurs when social norms are rejected on the basis that other higher norms are more pressing or important; for example, the murder of the abortion doctor could be neutralized on the grounds that God does not mean for innocent babies to be killed

**attachment:** believed to be the most important element of Hirschi's bonding theory; through attachments to conventional others an individual begins to develop "stakes in conformity"; the attachment can be to parents, school, religion, or even peers

**autonomy:** one of the six focal concerns that Walter Miller argues makes up the value system of the competing subculture; refers to the notion that lower-class youths seek freedom from external intervention and control

**belief:** element of Hirschi's bonding theory that refers to the internalizing of the conventional norms and values; conformity would then depend on the strength of a person's belief

**code of the street:** term used by Elijah Anderson to explain the disproportionate amount of violence among young African American males

**commitment:** element of Hirschi's bonding theory that refers to investing in conventional goals and norms; Hirschi argued that a person weighs the consequences of actions before acting, and if a person has higher "stakes in conformity," he or she would then have more to lose

**condemnation of the condemners:** technique of neutralization identified by Sykes and Matza; refers to shifting focus from actions of the offender to the motives or behaviors of the accuser

**control theories:** have a dim view of human nature; argue that people naturally set out to pursue self-interests, and conformity comes only through controlled social existence; these types of theories also assume value consensus even if an individual is violating those values

**cultural deviance:** also known as *culture conflict*; refers to the conflict that occurs as a result of two competing value systems coming into contact

**cultural transmission:** term used to refer to the passing on of a particular set of values or norms of a group over time

**culture conflict:** theoretical perspective that asserts that conflicting values systems coming into contact with one another may be the cause of delinquent or criminal behavior

**denial of injury:** one type of technique of neutralization used to excuse the behavior of the offender; specifically, this refers to the claim that no real harm was done by the deviant act

**denial of responsibility:** one type of technique of neutralization that extends the legal concept of intent to dismiss responsibility for deviant actions; statements such as "it was an accident" or "I couldn't help it" may be used to neutralize the deviant act

**denial of victim:** one type of technique of neutralization that denies the existence of a victim, thereby dismissing the wrongfulness of the deviant act

**differential association:** theory postulated by Edwin Sutherland that asserts criminal behavior is learned from intimate groups; learning the techniques of deviant acts and the accompanying value system that allows a person to engage in deviant acts are both necessary in order to become a criminal

**differential identification:** variation of the learning theory that specifies the degree of identity with a person as the key to adoption of the values making it more likely that a person will engage in criminal activity or norm abiding behavior

**drift:** concept developed by David Matza that argues that perhaps a soft deterministic view better explains criminal involvement; a person may drift in and out of criminal activity based upon the environmental and social factors that affect him or her

**excitement:** a focal concern identified by Walter Miller that refers to the need to engage in emotion-arousing entertainment that most often times violates the conventional norms

**fate:** a focal concern identified by Walter Miller that refers to the belief that one has little or no control over the forces that shape life

**focal concerns:** the six prominent values that Walter Miller identified within lower-class males; he proposes that in place of the conventional goals of society, the lower class supplant the focal concerns, which then become the dominant value system for the subculture

**general theory of crime:** Gottfredson and Hirschi's theory intended to explain all crime and founded on the notion that low self-control is the primary cause, that it is shaped by age eight, and that it remains stable throughout the life course

**hogging:** the practice of targeting overweight women for sexual exploitation

**involvement:** component of Hirschi's bonding theory that refers to the amount of time that an individual invests in the activities that create the "stakes in conformity" to conventional society

**learning theories:** view crime as "normal" rather than "pathological" due to the means in which criminal behavior develops; propose that criminal behavior is learned in much the same way as noncriminal behavior

**primary culture conflict:** aspect of culture conflict theory that refers to the collision of norms from different cultural systems

**secondary culture conflict:** aspect of culture conflict theory that refers to the collision of norms due to the evolution of subcultures within a heterogeneous society

**self control:** is said to be originated in early childhood, fixed by age 8, and constant across the life span; Gottfredson and Hirschi argue that the cause of all crime is low self control

**shared misunderstandings:** element of Matza's drift explanation that refers to the erroneous beliefs of young males that their peers are committed to delinquency

**smartness:** focal concern described by Walter Miller as the skills and abilities necessary to dominate verbal exchanges pertinent to lower-class environments

**social bond theory:** theory developed by Travis Hirschi that focuses attention on the ties to society or the "stakes in conformity" that prevent most people from engaging in delinquent behavior; assumes a very negative view of human nature; Hirschi identifies four components: attachment, commitment, involvement, and belief that describe the process of forming bonds with conventional society; he argues that once these bonds become weak or broken, deviant behavior is most likely to occur

**social control theories:** say that the propensity for crime or delinquency is a function of social processes that are assumed or delineated

**social learning theory:** belief that the techniques and skills necessary to engage in deviant behavior can be learned in a social context

**social process theories:** shift focus from macro-level theory to micro-level theory in an attempt to explain how individuals become law violators and what factor the social environment plays in the process; these theories do not assume that crime is a lower-class problem and try to explain crime across all social classes

**social psychological theories:** seeks to integrate micro-level and macro-level explanations of crime, social and psychological explanations, and account for crime across all social classes

**soft determinism:** concept put forth by David Matza that proposes that individuals may have a propensity to engage in deviant behavior and, depending on the environment this condition can lay dormant or become exacerbated

**subculture of violence:** refers to the research done by Marvin Wolfgang and Franco Ferracuti on spontaneous homicide and assault; they identify a subculture based on a notion of honor that resorts to violence and displays of physical aggression in order to defend honor

**symbolic interactionism:** concept that a person will conduct himself or herself according to the meaning that things have for them; people get definitions of their social environment through a process of interaction with that environment

**tautological:** true by virtue of its logical form alone

**techniques of neutralization:** means by which people generate a rationale to excuse law violation prior to violating because they fundamentally believe in the law

**toughness:** one of the focal concerns identified by Walter Miller that refers to the distorted image of masculinity; lower-class youths emphasize strength, physical prowess, and bravery over other qualities such as intellect and sensitivity

**trouble:** one of the focal concerns identified by Walter Miller that refers to interference from official social control agents of conventional society

## Key Criminologists

**Ronald Akers:** contemporary social learning theorist who expanded Sutherland's differential association theory to include some aspects of behaviorism

**Donald R. Cressey:** student of Edwin Sutherland who continued editing the next six editions of *Criminology* after Sutherland's death; Cressey did not alter the differential association theory after the death of Sutherland because he felt that it should be subjected to extensive testing prior to modification

**Franco Ferracuti:** along with Marvin Wolfgang he conducted extensive research into the subcultures and formulated a theory on a subculture of violence that relies on a notion of honor and resorts to violence in order to protect ad maintain that honor

**Daniel Glaser:** developed a variation of learning theory called *differential identification*; his theory looked at the degree of identity with a person, either real or imagined, as the most important element in the value adoption process

**Michael Gottfredson:** with Travis Hirschi, developed the general theory of crime that has been subject to wide debate and some empirical testing since 1990

**Travis Hirschi:** very prominent and influential criminologist who developed the social bond theory; his theory has been extensively tested and empirically supported; his bonding theory maintains that through bonds to society an individual is pressured to conform to the value system of that society; Hirschi identified four elements of social bond; he more recently developed the general theory of crime with Michael Gottfredson

**David Matza:** important criminologist who studied behavior patterns of young males; his observations of juveniles led him to the formulation of the neutralization theory; along with Gresham Sykes, he outlines the five techniques of neutralization that were commonly used to sidestep the mainstream society value system and allow for deviant behavior

**Walter Miller:** subculture criminologist who believed that the lower class did not subscribe to mainstream social norms and, in fact, had six focal concerns that prevailed in all aspects of their lives

**Thorsten Sellin:** culture conflict theorist who identified primary and secondary culture conflict; he fought to have the field of criminology move from a strict legalistic definition of crime to a more normative definition; he saw a strictly legal definition as being inadequate to explain laws of human nature

**Edwin H. Sutherland:** highly influential criminologist who developed differential association theory of crime; he was instrumental in moving the field of criminology away from the positivist school of thought to a more of a soft determinism perspective; his theory is delineated in a series of nine principles

**Gresham Sykes:** prominent criminologist who along with David Matza developed the neutralization theory

**Gabriel Tarde:** French criminologist whose theory, "laws of imitation," became influential in the development of Sutherland's differential association theory

**Charles Tittle:** criminologist whose research contributed to empirical and conceptual clarity in the early phases of contemporary deterrence research; conducted extensive research and testing of the differential association model proposed by Edwin Sutherland; his research as focused on the deficiencies in the causal framework set out by Sutherland; a chief opponent of labeling theory; Tittle claims that propositions of the labeling perspective are not clearly identified so as to allow for empirical research and believes the theory to be too vague

**Marvin Wolfgang:** prominent theorist in the area of subcultural explanations of crime; worked closely with Franco Ferracuti to develop the subculture of violence explanation of crime; they identified a subculture that deviated from conventional society in that it was founded on a notion of honor and, within this subculture, violence was an expected response in order to protect and secure this honor

# Chapter 9
# Social Reaction Theories of Crime

## Summary

Social reaction theories of crime focus on the formal and informal responses to the individual. This perspective is less concerned with the initial delinquent act or behavior and more concerned about the effects of the reaction of society to the individual. Social reaction theorists believe that the type of reaction given by society can influence further involvement in deviant acts and behaviors. In addition, social reaction theorists are interested not only in the formal response by society to individual acts, but also the response to an individual based upon other social factors such as age, demeanor of the individual, and physical characteristics.

## Labeling Theory

Labeling theory is associated with an earlier concept known as *symbolic interactionism*. Labeling theorists emphasize individual levels of behavior and are more concerned with the reaction from society. A major premise that labeling theory is based upon is the idea that criminal behavior is only "criminal" after it receives negative reaction from society. Labeling theorists argue that a formal response from the criminal justice system may exacerbate and encourage further delinquent behavior. Labeling is based upon the premise that conduct is not inherently deviant, but is differentially defined as deviant according to the context of particular social settings.

Theorists such as Frank Tannenbaum, Edwin Lemert, Howard Becker, and Edwin Schur describe the labeling cycle. The initial deviant act is responded to by society in a negative fashion. This negative reaction causes individuals to react in one of two ways: They tailor their behavior to elicit positive reactions from society, or they further engage in deviant acts. The introduction of the individuals into the system is described by Tannenbaum as the dramatization of evil. Edwin Lemert argues that this introduction and stronger penalties and rejection can lead to secondary deviation. Howard Becker addresses the concern of formal introduction into the system as a form of status degradation and believes that when this occurs, a changing of the master status to criminal is inevitable. Edwin Schur was more concerned with the effects of labeling on the juvenile offenders. He advocated that no action should be taken against juveniles and that society needed to take a more tolerant stance against juvenile delinquency. He maintains that formal introduction of juveniles into the system causes insurmountable obstacles for juveniles who later wish to break out of the cycle.

Charles Tittle criticized the labeling perspective, citing two specific problems. First, he argues that ambiguous propositions and premises of the theory make empirical research difficult to achieve. Second, limited data exist to support the labeling theory because it is so difficult to operationalize the concept in order to conduct research. Some available research, however, does seem to support the claims of the labeling perspective. One important policy implication directly related to labeling theory is system diversion and net widening. If formal responses to deviant behavior are to be avoided, would an alternative such as system diversion be susceptible to abuse and prone to net widening? The limited research seems to offer contradictory evidence. Some programs have experienced net widening while other programs seem not to have been affected.

## Social Conflict Theory

This perspective operates on a different assumption than do the social structure theories or social process theories. Social conflict theory approaches criminal behavior from a conflict as opposed to a consensus perspective. Conflict theorists believe that norms do not reflect a consensus of society to protect the community, but rather are the outcome of competing interest groups with those holding the most power defining norms. Norms are merely a way to further promote the interests of the groups that maintain power and status.

Karl Marx and Friedrich Engels are two chief proponents of conflict theory. The writings of Karl Marx, George Vold, Austin Turk, Richard Quinney, and William Chambliss have been extremely influential in the development of "conflict," "Marxist," "radical," and "critical" criminology. Marx maintained that the mode of production of capitalistic society influenced law and society. He believed that the powerful controlled the mode of production and that the law was a tool the wealthy used to further their interests and protect their investments.

George Vold was instrumental in the development of the group conflict theory. He saw society as a collection of groups, each with its own interests. Some groups form alliances because the members have common interests that can better be served through collective action. Vold maintains that as these groups encounter conflict, the resolution of said conflicts strengthens and intensifies the loyalty of the group. This can be a powerful tool for the state to manipulate.

Austin Turk believed that people were inherently neutral. He felt that they were neither good nor bad, but argued that those who maintained the power of a society had the ability to criminalize behaviors of those without power. This process of criminalization is dependent on five social factors: congruence of norms, level of organization, degree of sophistication, power differential between enforcers and violators, and the realism of moves during the conflict.

Richard Quinney viewed crime as the product of social definition. His social reality of crime proposed six propositions that supported his contention that in the stratified social system, a group's behavior becomes judged and condemned by another dominant and more powerful group. He emphasized that political power is necessary to establish and label criminal behavior. Without the backing of the dominant group, little will be done to enforce the law.

Through their analysis of the American justice system, William Chambliss and Robert Seidman dispelled the premises held by the consensus perspective. They found that law is not an accurate depiction of the values of society and, in fact, serves to promote the interests of powerful groups. They found that appellate court judges operate to ensure that the courts are more available to the wealthy and powerful than to the poor. Chambliss' law of vagrancy research also supports the contention that law exists to promote the interests of special groups and not the whole of society.

## Left Realism

This emerging area of radical criminology is focusing on the detrimental effects intraclass and intrarace crime have on the overall crime picture. They argue that although "suite" crime is important to the accurate depiction of the crime picture, nonetheless street crime is also important. In recent years, the trend has been to focus on white-collar crime, and the left realism perspective argues that the system needs to focus on both equally. There needs to be attention given to crimes of the wealthy and to crimes committed by the poor against the poor. Left realists do not romanticize street criminals as have some radical criminologists, but remain sensitive to causal forces rooted in the inequitable distribution of power that generates street crime.

This perspective leads into another emerging category of criminal justice, the human-ecological perspective. Led by theorist Elliott Currie, this perspective contends that the system needs to provide policy interventions at the individual, family, and the larger social level. He advocates addressing the problems that are exacerbating the class distinctions and promoting changes in the social institutions to raise the impoverished out of their despair. He recommends programs such as Head Start, expanded health and mental health services, better pre- and postnatal care, accessible nonpunitive drug abuse treatment programs, and increasing the minimum wage to reduce the inequality of the socially impoverished.

## Feminism

Gender provides a major basis of conflict as seen by all feminists. There are three major variations of feminist thought: radical, Marxist, and socialist.

## Postmodernism

This recent paradigm rejects the notion that "modern" science provides an objective way to seek understanding. It is argued that the "truth" is not so objective and can be sought in many ways. Language is seen as the key to power.

## Key Terms

**conflict perspective:** a perspective in contrast to the consensus view, and viewing society as comprised of various competing groups; the laws and values of the society are developed in order to further the interests of the groups that have the most power

**conformist:** a person who abides by the norms and laws of a society and is perceived by society as abiding by the norms and laws; a conformist is someone who does not wish to upset the status quo

**consensus view:** a perspective based upon the underlying assumption that laws and values in a society are developed through agreement of most members and groups of that society; this perspective believes that the state serves to protect the interest of the general public and society as a whole

**criminalization:** the process of being labeled criminal or labeling particular behaviors as criminal; conflict theorists believe that this occurs due to the law-breaking behavior, interaction, and exchange between law enforcers and the law breakers, as well as other social forms

**critical criminology:** a perspective viewing crime as a product of conflict among interest groups; it may take a variety of more specific views

**deconstructionism:** a postmodern view that knowledge derived from the scientific enterprise is not necessarily valid and must first be critiqued or discarded before proceeding to seek the "truth" in other ways

**deviance amplification:** the concept that once a label is applied to an individual especially by formal agents, as others become aware of the formal label they will begin to impose negative reactions on the individual as well

**dramatization of evil:** the process of social reaction to an individual who has been caught and labeled as a law violator; Frank Tannenbaum coined this concept in his 1938 publication *Crime and the Community*; the negative reaction to the specific act of the individual begins to be directed toward the individual as a person as well

**falsely accused:** people who conform to the norms of society, but are not perceived by society as doing so; this false perception can be based on factors other than behavior and activity; it can be based on factors such as style of dress, manner of speaking, or associates

**feminism:** a perspective that views the placement of women in the social structure as the key to understanding crime and other social problems

**group conflict theory:** belief that the origin of criminal behavior comes from the role of conflict between competing groups and the desire of one group to impose its values and power over others; the perspective was developed by George Vold

**instrumental Marxism:** a version of Marxism that sees the state as closely controlled by the power elite

**labeling perspective:** reaction to law violators by a society that deems certain behavior deviant, but in so doing amplifies the behavior; this perspective contrasts to the presumption of deterrence theory that punishment reduces deviant behavior; labeling theorists contend that there should be less punitive measures taken against law/norm violators to prevent them from acquiring a "criminal" label

**left realism:** branches off from the Marxist perspective; left realism views intraclass crime as a very significant problem that must be addressed; this group is especially concerned with victimization of minorities by members of their own group

**legal relativism:** the concept that acts are neither inherently good nor bad, but are varying levels of good and bad; it is the context in which an act is performed and the social reaction to it that determines whether it will be deemed acceptable or unacceptable; thus, labeling theorists maintain that no acts are inherently evil, but are defined according to time, place, and context

**Marxist criminology:** division of "conflict" criminology closely tied into the writings of Karl Marx; this perspective focuses on the definition of crime and has an emphasis on economic factors

**Marxist feminism:** sees women as economically dominated by men

**master status:** the characteristics that define the individual; an individual may have a master status of "doctor," "student," or "criminal" that provides the primary context in which people react to them

**moral entrepreneurs:** term coined by Howard Becker; moral entrepreneurs believe that their moral values are superior to those of others and attempt to impose these values on others by crusading to have their moral values adopted by society to make it a better place for its citizens

**net widening:** refers to the expansion of the scope of the criminal just system; system diversion began as an alternative to reduce the number of people labeled by introduction into the criminal justice apparatus, but opponents argue that those who normally would not have been brought into the system enter through diversion programs; thus, the number of persons negatively labeled is increased by alternative programs

**postmodernism:** a view of understanding the world that envisions "truth" as subjective and thus calls for many methods of seeking it; the scientific method as the dominant "modern" methodology is particularly critiqued

**primary deviation:** the original deviant behavior of persons negatively labeled; Edwin Lemert identified this as the starting point in a counterproductive labeling process; primary deviance only occasional, experimental, or a product of many different causal factors

**pure deviant:** a person who engages in norm-violating behavior and is accurately perceived by society as doing so

**radical criminology:** relies upon the philosophy of Karl Marx; this perspective advocates the involvement in ongoing political struggles and questions the legal definitions of crime

**radical feminism:** sees a patriarchal social order at the root of crime and other problems

**radical nonintervention:** a concept introduced by Edwin Schur maintaining that the less that is done with children who deviate, the more likely they are to reform; this concept is congruent with the assumptions of the labeling perspective, the belief is that punishment of violating youths serves only to label them and isolate them from legitimate roles

**retrospective interpretation:** the concept that a person's behavior is reinterpreted in light of new information introduced about that individual; once a label has been acquired, a person's behavior may be reinterpreted in light of the newly acquired label

**secondary deviation:** introduced by Edwin Lemert, this element of the labeling perspective refers to continuation of primary deviant behaviors that can no longer be explained away or excused by society; as a defense, attack, or adjustment to the reaction from society, this involves continued engagement in activities and behaviors that violate social norms or laws

**secret deviant:** a person who engages in norm-violating behavior but is not perceived by society as such; he or she is often able to escape the detection of law enforcers or society

**social conflict theory:** focuses on the roles played by political, economic, and other social institutions in the shaping of societal definitions of legal and illegal behaviors

***Social Pathology:*** book written by Edwin Lemert in 1951; in this book, Lemert developed the primary and secondary deviation distinctions

**socialist feminism:** sees women, along with other groups, as inevitably oppressed by capitalism

**structural Marxism:** a version of Marxism that sees the state and criminal law as relatively autonomous from the power elite

## Key Criminologists

**Howard S. Becker:** prominent proponent of labeling perspective in the 1960s; wrote *Outsiders: Studies in the Sociology of Deviance* in 1963; coined the term "moral entrepreneur"

**William Chambliss:** a conflict criminologist who co-wrote *Law, Order and Power* with Robert Seidman; they examined legal subsystems and traced the law in action; they concluded that the law in action does not represent the interests of society at large but rather represents the interests of those in power

**Edwin Lemert:** wrote *Social Pathology* in 1951 and contributed to the concept of primary and secondary deviation to the labeling perspective; he argued that formal response to deviant acts and criminal activities would most likely cause further involvement in the activities

**Karl Marx:** German economist and social philosopher who was highly critical of the consensus perspective and the capitalist structure; his writings have laid the groundwork for the development of conflict theories in criminology; Karl Marx claims that it is the mode of production that influences the laws and values of society

**Richard Quinney:** a renowned critical criminologist responsible for developing the social reality of crime theory wherein he outlined six propositions he believed explained crime and criminal behavior; he sees crime as the product of social definition

**Edwin M. Schur:** wrote *Radical Nonintervention* in 1973, arguing that society needed to take a more tolerant stance toward norm-violating youths; he believed that labeling youths was counterproductive and served to isolate them from legitimate roles in society

**Robert Seidman:** believes that law in action does not represent the public interest, but in actuality represents the interests of the groups who maintain power; co-wrote *Law, Order and Power* with William Chambliss

**Frank Tannenbaum:** wrote *Crime and the Community* in 1938, in which he developed such concepts as dramatization of evil and legal relativism; he was interested in what transpired with individuals after they had been labeled norm violators

**Charles R. Tittle:** criminologist whose research contributed to empirical and conceptual clarity in the early phases of contemporary deterrence research; conducted extensive research and testing of the differential association model proposed by Edwin Sutherland; his research has focused on the deficiencies in the causal framework set out by Sutherland; chief opponent of labeling theory; Tittle claims that propositions of the labeling perspective are not clearly identified so as to allow for empirical research and believes the theory to be too vague

**Austin Turk:** wrote Criminality and Legal Order in 1969, which claimed that criminality is contextual; the people with the power to label behavior as "criminal" do so at the expense of those who have no power; developed the concept of criminalization

**George Vold:** a leading conflict criminologist who was instrumental in developing the group conflict perspective

Chapter 10
# Recent Developments in Criminological Theory

## Summary

Integrated theoretical models, criminal career research, and developmental criminology are several of the current approaches to understanding crime that have been on the cutting edge during the past decade. An acceptance of limitations of existing theories has encouraged integrated theoretical models. Research findings that indicate a violent and criminally active group of offenders that account for more than half of all street crime has been instrumental in the development of a career criminal explanation. Developmental criminology resulted from a combination of both integrated theoretical models and criminal career research.

## Integrated Theoretical Models

This model attempts to combine and fuse existing theoretical approaches in order to more fully explain the causes of crime. Existing theories standing alone do not account for a considerable amount of the variation in crime rates, so it is the objective of integrated models to combine existing theories in order to account for a greater amount of variation in crime rates.

Some early attempts at integrated theoretical models can be illustrated in Shaw and McKay's social ecological theory. Shaw and McKay integrated both social disorganization and social learning theories. Cloward and Ohlin's differential opportunity theory integrates strain theory with social learning theory. Despite theoretical integration's introduction as far back as the 1940s, it was not until the 1970s that the approach began to spur the serious attention of the criminological field.

A major question to be addressed before the integrated approach can be accepted is whether, in fact, different theories can actually be combined. In order for an integrated model to work, it is absolutely essential that theories be analyzed and examined for underlying assumptions. A successful fusing of theories depends on whether any given theories have compatible underlying assumptions. A major mistake that is sure to end in failure would be to attempt to integrate theories that are inherently incompatible at their basic levels.

Some criminologists are vehemently opposed to theory integration. Travis Hirschi contends that "separate is better"; Delbert Elliott maintains that there can be a "reconciliation of different assumptions."

## Approaches to Integration

The most common approach to theory integration is the end-to-end model. Theories are combined in a sequential model so that one theory winds up being temporally more proximate to the actual act than the other theories. The end-to-end model suggests that one theory best explains early causes of delinquency and another theory best explains the proximate act or actual precipitating factors.

## Objectives of Integration

The field of criminology is experiencing a surge in integrated models to explain crime due to an increased statistical sophistication that was introduced into the social sciences in the 1950s and 1960s. Tests such as multiple regression analysis make an integrated explanation of crime more feasible, and a more accurate picture can be obtained as to the amount of variance a particular theory explains. Another reason why integrated models are experiencing such interest has to do with the dissatisfaction with current theories in explaining a significant amount of variance in crime.

## Elliott, Ageton, and Cantor—
## An Integrated Theoretical Perspective

This integrated model combines aspects of strain, social learning, and social control into a single explanatory paradigm. Using self-reports, these researchers believe that it is possible to identify individuals that are involved in habitual criminal activity. The Elliott et al. model is an example of an end-to-end approach. An important finding of their research is that multiple paths lead to both delinquent and nondelinquent behavior.

## Colvin and Pauly—An Integrated Structural-Marxist Theory of Delinquency Production

This integrated model introduces a structural-Marxist theory that integrates elements of the micro-sociological theories. They maintain that capitalism and its accompanying social relations to the means of production produce different attitudes toward authority. Colvin and Pauly claim that based upon the type of social control workers experience in the workforce, they can either develop positive or negative reactions toward authority. This experience is reproduced at home and, in turn, is the source for orientation for adolescents, as well.

## Ogle, Maier-Katkin, and Bernard— Homicidal Behavior Among Women

This theory integrates a number of perspectives to explain homicide among all classes of women. It focuses particularly on the strains caused by the female role and the social control of women. It is consistent with both the low homicide rate of women and the patterns of such homicide.

## Tittle—Control Balance Theory

This integrated theory combines elements of control and routine activities theories. At the heart of this theory is the idea of "control balance." Tittle believes that deviance occurs when there is an imbalance between the amount of control that can be exercised and the amount of control to which one is subjected.

## Tests of Integrated Models

Most research supports the basic contention that integrated models account for higher rates of explanation of variance for crime. Further research indicates that the ability of a given model to explain behavior varies according to the type of behavior in question. Social learning/social control theories seem to better explain variation in delinquency.

## Policy Relevance of Integrated Models

Some possible policy recommendations advanced by integrated models include parent education classes to teach parents how better to discipline, monitor, and socialize their children. Some others are the furthering economic support for programs such as Head Start or the Perry Preschool Program. The structural-Marxist model may advocate policies and programs designed to reduce inequality in society and improve the conditions currently found in the labor market.

## The Criminal Career Debate

Some criminologists support the claim that criminals can be separated into two groups: active offenders and non-offenders. Opponents to such a position claim this distinction is artificial and people in fact vary in their degree of "crime proneness." Much of the criminal career research dates back to work conducted by Sheldon and Eleanor Glueck during the 1930s and 1940s. The Gluecks gathered data from 500 delinquent boys and matched 400 nondelinquent boys. In their research, the Gluecks identified descriptive characteristics of delinquent versus nondelinquent offenders.

Marvin Wolfgang resurrected the Glueck's research and conducted research that further fueled the knowledge pool of the criminal career debate. Other contributors include Nagin and Land, Alfred Blumstein, Jacqueline Cohen, David Farrington, and Arnold Barrett. The chief opponents of the criminal career claim include Travis Hirschi, and Michael Gottfredson, who believe that low self-control is the basis for criminal propensity.

The criminal career position offers only limited support for the incapacitative model and the current "three strikes, you're out" notion. Proponents of the criminal career maintain that life events such as marriage, divorce, parenthood, employment, and unemployment have significant impacts on patters of offending. It is the "career criminal" who is targeted most directly by incapacitation efforts.

## Policy Relevance of the Criminal Career Paradigm

The premise supporting the criminal career paradigm is that incarcerating identified offenders during their periods of high offending would reduce crime. This whole premise is popular given the current social atmosphere wherein a "get tough" on crime stance is prevalent. If high-risk offenders were to be identifiable and incapacitated during the periods where they had a high risk of offending, it could save hundreds of millions of dollars in taxpayers' money.

## Developmental and Life-Course Criminology

This approach is concerned with two aspects of criminal behavior. First, this perspective is concerned with the dynamics of problem behaviors and offending with age. Second, it is concerned with identifying causal factors that predate and co-occur with the behavioral development. This perspective focuses on macro-level correlates as well as individual patterns of behavior.

A major question that the developmental criminologist seeks to explain is whether the higher rates of criminal activity present in adolescents is indicative of a higher prevalence rate or a higher individual offending rate. Research seems to indicate that the increase in adolescent criminal activity is due to a larger number of offenders rather than an increase in the criminal activities of a few offenders.

## Sampson and Laub's Developmental Model

These two criminologists have formulated their developmental model of criminal behavior based on a reexamination of earlier data provided by Sheldon and Eleanor Glueck. This model is grounded in social control theory assuming that criminal behavior is the manifestation of weak or attenuated bonds to society. They found evidence to support the assertion that strong social bonds are critical for preventing delinquency. If strong social bonds exist during adolescence but are weakened or broken later in life, the individual may be set on a course for offending. Likewise, an adolescent who has weak or broken bonds to society may later develop strong social bonds and thus engaging in criminal activity will be less likely.

## Key Terms

**adolescent-limited:** within developmental criminology, these are the normally healthy adolescents who mimic antisocial behavior but usually fail to continue that sort of behavior into adulthood

**career criminal:** also known as a *habitual offender*; this type of offender is the target of "three-strikes" legislation

**criminal career:** refers to the sequence of offending during sometime period; involves a beginning, duration at some measurable level, and a period of inactivity or termination

**discontinuity:** the period of inactivity in a criminal career, often marking the termination of criminal offending

**duration:** in a criminal career, this refers to the length of time an offender engages in criminal activity, usually measured by is frequency or lambda

**end-to-end model:** the most common approach to an integrated theoretical model; theories are combined in a sequential fashion so that one theory ends up being temporally more proximate to the actual act than the other theories

**frequency:** a level of measurement for criminal career

**initiation:** signals the beginning of a criminal career; it is important for this to be identified so that an accurate measure of duration can be obtained and future criminal activity can be predicted

**integrated model approach:** a combining of existing theoretical approaches in order to more fully understand and explain crime

**lambda:** a level of measurement of the frequency of offending during a criminal career

**latent trait:** refers to a person's "crime proneness"; assumed by some that the presence of this is associated with an increased likelihood that the individual will engage in criminal behavior

**life-course persistent:** within developmental criminology, this group displays pathological antisocial tendencies resulting in criminal offending

**maintenance:** according to criminologist Alfred Blumstein, refers to the period of time after initiation and before the termination of a criminal career in which the offender is involved in criminal activity

**onset:** refers to the beginning of criminal involvement marking the initiation of a criminal career

**patterned delinquent activity:** according to the Elliott model, this is the most important variable to focus on when discussing the causes and correlates of delinquency

**termination:** the period of inactivity in a criminal career usually marking the end of such career

**three strikes:** refers to current legislation that mandates automatic life sentences for third-time violent offenders

## Key Criminologists

**Alfred Blumstein:** most vocal proponent of the criminal career paradigm, along with Jacqueline Cohen and David Farrington; he argues that there are different explanatory models for the initiation, maintenance, and termination of criminal activity

**Jacqueline Cohen:** criminologist who recently has contributed to criminal career research; vocal proponent of the criminal career paradigm, along with Alfred Blumstein and David Farrington

**Mark Colvin:** along with John Pauley, developed an integrated structural-Marxist theory to explain juvenile delinquency; the key variables of the theory are parents; social class and the coerciveness of the parents' workplace social control structure; their theory combined control theories, opportunity theories, and social learning theories

**Delbert Elliott:** along with Suzanne Ageton and Rachelle Canter, combined strain, social learning, and social control theories to explain patterned delinquent behavior

**David Farrington:** conducted a longitudinal study in England that tested properties of developmental criminology; his research concluded that the increase in juvenile crime rates is attributable to an increase in the number of offenders rather than an increase in criminal activity of a small number of offenders; vocal proponent of the criminal career paradigm, along with Alfred Blumstein and Jacqueline Cohen

**Michael Gottfredson:** collaborating with Travis Hirschi, put forth an explanation of crime that asserts that it is the product of a single underlying construct—identified as low self-control

**Travis Hirschi:** developed social bonding theory; he is opposed to an integrationist approach, arguing that assumptions of the different types of theories are fundamentally incompatible

**Julie Horney:** involved in criminal career research; identified a violent and/or highly criminal group of offenders but has not produced any prediction instrument to identify these individuals; research suggests importance of social events on the rate of offending

**David Huizinga:** influential criminologist who has conducted extensive research in hope of finding how to identify serious or career offenders; his work has focused predominantly on youths and more specifically the multiple paths to becoming delinquent, testing to see if race of class differences are factors correlated with increased juvenile delinquent involvement

**Marvin Krohn:** along with Terence Thornberry, published an overview of the major findings from seven longitudinal studies

**John Laub:** collaborated with Robert Sampson to formulate the developmental model of criminal behavior; using secondary data gathered by the Gluecks in their book *Unraveling Juvenile Delinquency*, they studied the within-individual change over time while acknowledging the importance of life transitions to understanding behavioral patterns

**Rolf Loeber:** among the developmental criminologists who have found evidence to support the observation that some youths do not continue their antisocial behavior into adolescence while other youths who had no prior history of antisocial behavior during childhood begin to engage in such activities during the adolescent years

**Ross Matsuedo:** undertook delinquency research, concluding that when differential association is properly operationalized it accounts for more than 50 percent of the variation in reported delinquency and mediates the effects of the social control variable

**Joan McCord:** developmental criminologist who conducted research on within-individual change over time of delinquent activity; she notes that a majority of adolescents cease delinquent activity during their early adult years and recognizes that a significant proportion of adult criminals have no record of delinquency during adolescence

**Terrie Moffitt:** developmental criminologist that proposed that two distinct categories of offenders exist: the adolescent-limited and the life-course persistent; she further argues that these two categories have distinct etiologies that require separate analysis

**John Pauly:** prominent criminologist who along with Mark Colvin developed an integrated structural Marxist theory to explain juvenile delinquency

**Lee Robins:** developmental criminologist whose research supports the observation that some children do not continue antisocial behavior into adolescence, while some youths with no history of childhood problems become involved in delinquent activities during adolescence

**Robert Sampson:** conducted research with John Laub and proposed a developmental model of criminal behavior

**Terence Thornberry:** through research testing interaction theory, concluded that theory should choose neither differential association/learning theory nor control theory and suggests further research focus on the reciprocal relationship

**Charles R. Tittle:** criminologist whose research contributed to empirical and conceptual clarity in the early phases of contemporary deterrence research; conducted extensive research and testing of the differential association model proposed by Edwin Sutherland; his research has focused on the deficiencies in the causal framework set out by Southerland; a chief opponent of labeling theory; Tittle claims that propositions of the labeling perspective are not clearly identified so as to allow for empirical research and believes the theory to be too vague

**Marvin Wolfgang:** important criminologist who has contributed significant research to the criminal career debate; his findings show that there is a small proportion of offenders committing a large majority of the offenses

# Chapter 11
# Violent Crime

## Summary

Violent crimes such as murders, robberies, rapes, and assaults are usually the ones that frighten people the most. The fear generated by these types of crimes has impact on many Americans. People become more cautious, avoid public transportation, stay indoors at night, and curb their recreational activities so that they will not have to return home after dark. Violence has permeated literature, cinema, and television. Children seem to be the most impressionable. Constant bombardment with violent stimuli is sure to be manifested in the way a child plays or interacts with other people.

Some anthropological studies have shown that humans are not innately violent. Violence is learned after birth in a social context. Johan Galtung believes that, as a society, the United States should focus its attention on reducing cultural violence. Until aspects of a culture that can be used to legitimize violence are addressed, violence will continue.

## Index Crimes: Homicide, Assault, and Rape

Homicide is one type of violent crime that most people often fear. It is known as the unlawful killing of a person by another with malice aforethought, occurring after the birth of the victim within one year and one day from the time the injury was inflicted. The criminal act itself does not necessarily have to be the only cause of death; it need only be a causal factor. The law mandates four categories of homicides: murder, manslaughter, excusable homicide, and justifiable homicide.

Each category of homicide is further broken down into varying degrees. For instance, premeditation and malice aforethought are elements necessary to prove first-degree murder. After the events of September 11, the legislature in New York added acts of terrorism to be included as first-degree murder. The felony-murder doctrine states that if a death occurs during the commission of a felony, the perpetrator can be charged with first-degree murder. Second-degree murder needs only to prove malice aforethought. First-degree manslaughter, or voluntary manslaughter, needs only to show that the defendant might have reasonably anticipated death as the outcome of the actions. Second-degree manslaughter and, in some cases, negligent manslaughter may include harm that occurred as a result of the specific action of the defendant (e.g., if a person was fatally wounded as a result of a fall during a fistfight). An excusable homicide is a death that occurs as a result of an accident where the "perpetrator" was obeying the law and exhibiting proper caution. Justifiable homicide includes the infliction of the death penalty and killing in self-defense.

There appears to be no consistent pattern for homicide in the United States. Research shows that the South has much higher violence reported than any other region of the United States. Subculture theories may best account for this phenomenon. Saturday seems to be the most likely day for murder, and research found that more than one-half of homicides take place in the home. In many homicides, a concern with "saving face" seems to be an important factor. Wolfgang introduced the concept of "victim-precipitation," where an escalation of violence seems to exacerbate confrontations between victim and attacker. He argues that in a victim-precipitated homicide, the victim was the first to invoke a violent response.

Mass murder and serial killings are an area of homicides undeserving of the proportion of the attention they receive. Contrary to what image is portrayed in the media, serial killings and mass murders represent a mere 1 or 2 percent of the annual homicide rate. Perhaps because these sorts of crimes are so shocking or, to some, intriguing, they continue to get a disproportionate share of media and public attention. Killers such as John Wayne Gacy, The Night Stalker, and Jeffrey Dahmer become trading-card celebrities, further heightening the allure of such a type of crime.

Some may argue that people who can kill must have some sort of mental deficiency, that they must be insane, or even that they must be "sick." Murderers in reality are merely a product of social forces. Americans seem to be held hostage to the fear of unprovoked stranger violence, when, in reality, research shows that a majority of all homicides are better understood as confrontational homicides. Sociologist Leonard Beeghley proposed five postulates for explaining the high homicide rate in the U.S.: (1) greater availability of guns; (2) the illegal drug market; (3) greater racial discrimination; (4) greater exposure of violence; and (5) greater economic inequality.

Despite the fear of the American people, homicide rates seem to be correlated with many social factors that could be negated using preventative measures. One factor that can lead to an increase in violence and homicides is economic inequality. Research seems to indicate that when a country has an area of severe poverty, then that area will usually experience higher violent confrontations or homicides. Some other factors that may be tied into homicide rates are alcohol consumption, drug usage, and (as some may argue) gun control.

## Assault and Battery

Assault is the threat or an attempt to do bodily harm to another; battery is the actual acts or physical conduct used to carry out those threats. Incidences where threats or attempts are completed are classified as simple assaults. If contact has been made with a victim in order to carry out those threats, then this is considered aggravated assault. Assault is classified as the most common violent crime: the Uniform Crime Reports show that approximately one million aggravated assaults occur annually, though victim surveys indicate that each year about one-half million assaults go unreported.

## Rape

The definition of rape has expanded in scope from just a violent crime against a female to a violent crime that includes homosexual rape, sexual assault of females upon males, and forced sexual activity other than penile-vaginal intercourse. A new area of concern that has come to the forefront of society's attention in the last two decades is that of marital rape. More than one-half of the states now have legislation that criminalizes marital rape. Of all the Index crimes listed in the Uniform Crime Reports, rape has shown the most dramatic increase.

Much of the current research on rape attempts to explain the motivation for such a violent crime. Girls younger than 18 years of age comprise more than one-half of the reported rapes. Current debate centers on whether the increase in rape rates can be attributed to an increase in reporting or whether the number of rapes has actually increased. The police and courts seem to be growing more sensitive to the needs of the rape victim, and this could explain the increase in reported rapes in the past decade.

Statistically, men are responsible for almost all the reported rapes, but women accused as accessories to the act constitute one percent. Rape seems to be predominantly an intraracial offense, with the 20- to 24-year-old category comprising the largest number of offenders. Research also shows that the pattern for rape does not mirror the pattern for all crimes in that rape rates do seem to vary directly with city size. There is a disproportional amount of lower class, minority, urban youth who experience an environment hospitable to violence. Some men see women as sex objects and use violence to achieve goals.

## Explaining Rape

Various explanations ranging from psychological to sociological apply to the violent crime of rape. An offender's psychological stability can lead an individual to commit rape due to a need to satisfy a quest for power, to satisfy anger, or to inflict injury upon others.

Feminist theory argues that rape occurs as a result of a long and deep-rooted social tradition where males have dominated political, social, and economic life. Social learning theorists view rape more as an acting out of the patterns of aggression that are reinforced through social stimuli. Sociobiological theory maintains that rape occurs as a result of men's low investment in the creation of offspring. The sociobiology theorist believes that rapists are attempting to father as many children as possible to ensure the continuation of their heritage.

## Family Violence

Interpersonal violence within families seems to frequently result in violent crimes such as murder, rape, and assault. These types of crimes are the least reported and least pursued by the criminal justice system. Child abuse, wife beating, violence toward siblings, and violence toward the elderly seem to be the most common types of family violence.

Child abuse, though not a new crime, became an issue in the forefront of American society with the assistance of physician C. Henry Kempe. Dr. Kempe's article "The Battered-Child Syndrome" helped provide an operational definition of the mistreatment of children. Current reference to child abuse is deemed "child maltreatment," which includes physical, emotional, and sexual abuse and neglect of the child within the scope of criminal mistreatment of children.

Wife beating is another highly personal issue that is moving to the forefront of American society. With the opening of battered women's shelters, more abused women have opted to leave the abusive environment and seek assistance. Police and the court systems have changed the way in which they resolve issues revolving around battered women and domestic violence.

Violence toward siblings and violence toward the elderly are two areas of concern with domestic violence debate. The largest number of cases of domestic violence takes place among siblings. Suzanne Steinmetz sees sibling violence perpetuating as a result of the toleration by parents of physical acts of aggression between and among children. Recently, attention has been turned to incidents of child-parent violence where mistreatment of aged parents includes physical abuse and failing to provide adequate care.

## Explaining Family Violence

Studies show that violence is most prevalent in lower-class homes. This could be contributed to by the stresses of poverty, welfare existence, poor housing and education, and limited opportunities. Some believe that violence is intergenerational and is passed on from one generation to the next. Conflict theorists see violence more in terms of the powerful and the powerless. Children and wives represent powerless roles in American society; therefore, they are unable to change the criminal code to criminalize such behavior.

## Corporate, Government, and Professional Violence

Equally as violent as other types of previously discussed crimes, yet virtually ignored or extensively downplayed in comparison, white-collar crime expands corporations, governments, and other professional areas of American society. White-collar crime is far more serious in terms of monetary and human life losses than street crime, yet it still virtually remains distant in the minds of many Americans. Governments can also commit violence upon their own citizens and those of foreign countries, with the United States being no exception. Physicians and the medical profession represent another area where violence can be hidden. Every year, unnecessary surgeries are performed, causing maiming, pain, suffering, and sometimes even death. Some theorists would argue that knowingly performing unnecessary surgeries would be tantamount to assault. The hallmark of organized crime is a willingness to resort to violence to gain an advantage. Organized crime may be related directly to anomie theory in that illegitimate/illegal means are used to achieve the goals of that organization. Until recently there has been a notable absence of African Americans in organized crime syndicates.

Most Americans regard deaths that occur as a result of corporations, government, and professionals as "accidents" and rationalize away the accountability. Moreover, research has found that American citizens regard white-collar crime with less concern than street crime. Current research seems to be indicating that a change is occurring. White-collar crime seems to be coming to the attention of the American public, and it is arousing much more concern among the public than it had previously.

## Key Terms

**assault and battery:** assault is a threat or an attempt to do bodily harm to another, while battery implies that the act was carried out

**battered-child syndrome:** term coined by C. Henry Kempe and colleagues in an article published in the *Journal of the American Medical Association* in 1962; the article "discovered" or brought child abuse to the public's attention; the term "battered-child syndrome" was used as the operational definition of the mistreatment of children diagnosed through pediatric radiology

**battered women:** also referred to as "wife beating"; describes women who are involved in a relationship in which the significant other uses violence as a response

**extortion:** the criminal offense of obtaining money or some other valuable item through the use of force or a threat of force if the payment is not delivered

**felony-murder:** a criminal offense in which the perpetrator is charged with murder if a death results from a specified felonious act; for example, if a victim of a burglary dies of a heart attack during the course of the burglary, then the burglar can be held responsible for the crime of murder

**homicide:** legally defined as the unlawful killing of one human being by another with malice aforethought, occurring after the birth of the victim resulting in the victim's demise not more than one year and one day from the time the injury was inflicted

**lifetime murder risk:** probability that a randomly selected person will become a murder victim over the course of that person's life span, assuming the murder rate remains stable; dependent on factors such as city size, region, and presence of drug/gang subcultures

**malice aforethought:** the actual act or manifestation of a deliberate intention to take the life of another human

**manslaughter:** a category of homicide lacking the element of malice aforethought; divided into two categories: voluntary and involuntary

**mass killers:** offenders who kill multiple victims in a single crime episode

**money laundering:** involves the transfer of funds from an illegal source to other accounts so that when the money comes back to the illegal possessor, that money appears to be legitimate income

**organized crime:** involves identifiable groups who often control drug smuggling and sales operations, illegal gambling, and similar activities; major organized crime groups often are identified by the term "mafia"

**premeditation:** refers to the prior formation or the preplanning of intent to kill

**relative deprivation:** refers to the belief that an individual will become resentful because his or her share of material goods seems slight compared to what others have or what is available

**serial killers:** offenders who repeat murders over a period of time

**sibling violence:** responsible for the largest number of domestic violence incidents; some criminologists argue that the condoning of violence between siblings does not reinforce positive conflict resolution skills and, in fact, serves as a training process that may carry over into later relationships in their lives

**victim precipitation:** introduced by Marvin Wolfgang; refers to the belief that a victim may be one of the precipitating factors encouraging his or her own victimization, usually be being the first to utilize physical violence

## Key Criminologists

**Scott Decker:** replicated the Marvin Wolfgang classic study of homicides in St. Louis; he found that more than 90 percent of homicides were intraracial events

**Jack Katz:** analyzed shoplifting accounts obtained from primarily female criminology students at UCLA; he found that material needs were inadequate to account for their thefts and believed that, for the students, shoplifting was a tactic in a war against boredom rather than against poverty

**Albert J. Reiss, Jr.:** conducted research on violence and crime; he concluded that most violent crimes occur over the course of a long criminal career dominated by property offenses and that serial murders make up only about one to two percent of the annual homicide rate

**Marvin Wolfgang:** important criminologist who has contributed significant research to the criminal career debate; in 1958, conducted a classic study of murder by analyzing police records for all homicides in Philadelphia during a 5-year period; introduced the concept of victim-precipitation

# Chapter 12
# Economic Crime

## Summary

The desire for others' property, and therefore the crime of theft, originates in cultural emphases. Theft is especially common when there is a heavy emphasis on material wealth but legitimate opportunities for acquiring it are limited. The American Dream places such an emphasis on wealth.

## Acquisitiveness and Theft

Crimes committed to gain money and goods are called *economic crimes*. Theft is not present in all societies. Murder is common among the natives in the interior of Papua, New Guinea, but cheating and theft are unknown concepts. Similarly, the Dakota and Navaho Indians had strong moral codes against the accumulation of wealth. In ancient Jewish and German law, theft was considered more serious and was dealt with more harshly than many violent crimes.

## The Law of Theft

Theft is divided into several specific forms. Larceny is taking a person's property without their consent and with the intent to deprive them of the property permanently. Larceny is further divided into grand and petit (petty) larceny, based on the value of the good stolen. However, this distinction has become blurred in recent years, and the FBI no longer divides larceny into separate categories.

Robbery involves the taking of property through the use of violence or fear. The fear must be "reasonable." There is no robbery if there is no resistance and the force consists of merely grabbing the property. Robbery is always considered more serious than larceny, regardless of the value of the property stolen. Robbery is often considered a violent crime.

Under common law, burglary is the breaking and entering of another's dwelling at night with the intent to commit a felony therein. Night, for this offense, was originally defined as any time when there was not enough light to discern a person's features. However, the hours that constitute night are now defined in the burglary statutes. The law has also extended burglary to cover similar crimes committed in the daytime and to buildings other than dwellings.

## Robbery

Certain psychological attributes are necessary for successful robbery. The task offers quicker rewards, but also the risks of personal confrontation. In fact, 10 percent of all homicides occur in the context of a robbery. Wright and Decker's interviews of St. Louis robbers revealed the safety concerns and the frequency of robbing other persons involved in crimes, such as sale of drugs.

## Burglary

Research has shown that target hardening, such as better locks and windows, does not deter burglary. Most burglars are proficient at dealing with the devices, and most homeowners do not use the devices effectively. Target hardening can also be a hazard to the homeowners if there should be a fire or other emergency requiring a quick exit from the home. Target-hardening devices can also attract burglars because they take it as an indication that there is something valuable inside.

The greatest deterrent to a burglar is the likelihood of being seen. Burglars therefore will rarely enter a house that is occupied. They are ingenious at discovering which houses are unoccupied. One method is to look for houses with the air conditioners turned off and the windows down on hot days.

Around eight percent of the households in the United States are burglarized annually. The southern states have the highest burglary rate; the northeastern states, the lowest. Males commit slightly over 90 percent of all burglaries. The rate of burglary in the United States has dropped approximately 44 percent since 1980. Rational choice theory is most often used to explain burglary.

## Shoplifting and Employee Theft

The extent of shoplifting in the United States is not known because stores blend losses from the activity into their inventory shrinkage. Apparently, theft comprises about 80 percent of inventory shrinkage, and employees perpetrate about 75 percent of the theft. In a study of college students who had shoplifted, Jack Katz concluded that the students stole because they were seeking a thrill rather than because they had an economic need.

## Telemarketing Fraud

Telemarketing becomes illegal when the seller oversteps the bounds of honesty, ignoring what has been established as acceptable limits of merchandising truthfulness. Of the estimated 140,000 telemarketing firms in existence in the United States today, approximately 10 percent engage in illegal activities. Americans lose about $40 billion a year to fraudulent sales pitches. However, because victims are sometimes embarrassed by their gullibility, only one in 10,000 victims will report their losses to authorities.

## Computer Crime

The National Center for Computer Crime Data reports that students and employees with access to a computer comprise the largest groups of computer criminals. Most losses are due to system and data damage, followed by theft and direct money loss. Computer criminals are usually sentenced to restitution. Computer crimes could have been punished under existing statutes, but legislators created special computer legislation in reaction to sensational cases presented by the media.

## White-Collar Economic Offenses

There is disagreement among criminologists about whether the concept of white-collar crime should be based on the characteristics of the offenders or the nature of the offenses. Although the term *white-collar crime* is relatively new, there were attempts to control business practices even in biblical times. To maintain control of corporations, they can exist only under charter from the state. Yet, most industrial regulations followed disasters rather than proactive analyses of problems.

Edwin H. Sutherland coined the term *white-collar crimes*. Noting that common theories of his time attributing crime to broken homes, Oedipal fixations, and poverty could not explain white-collar offenses, he assumed that his differential association theory would explain them. White-collar offenders typically claim that they stole only from companies that could afford the loss or blame their offenses on alcoholism, drug addiction, or marital problems. These reasoning processes are consistent with neutralization theory if they precede the criminal activity.

Most people do not realize when they have been victimized by white-collar crime. The offenses are usually diffused over a large group of people so that the loss to each individual is insignificant. Policing must be proactive to detect white-collar crimes because there are no complainants.

White-collar crime now receives much more attention: the misdeeds of the tobacco industry, Medicaid fraud, and a host of other recently discovered crimes. This focus has had considerable impact on the criminal justice system, though the fairness of prosecution and sentencing of white-collar offenders is heavily debated by criminologists.

## Key Terms

**American Dream:** the relentless push toward material success associated with anomie and related theories of crime

**booster box:** a device used by professional shoplifters, consisting of a parcel, often wrapped in paper or string, with a hidden spring trap that allows the thief to reach inside and open the bottom while it is resting on the merchandise to be stolen

**burglary:** under common law is defined as the breaking and entering of the dwelling house of another in the night with the intent to commit a felony therein; statutes have greatly extended the original common law scope of burglary to include warehouses, storehouses, offices, and similar structures

**criminaloid:** a person who is socioeconomically well-placed but commits crime, similar to the concept of white-collar crime

**fence:** a person who buys stolen goods from thieves to resell for profit

**grand larceny:** the taking of property from a person, without that person's consent and with the intent to deprive the person permanently of the use of the property; distinguished from petit larceny by the value of the property stolen, with grand larceny involving higher value

**inventory shrinkage:** a term used by stores that includes merchandise that is damaged and sold at a reduced price, bookkeeping errors, breakage, and employee thefts, as well as shoplifting losses; the best estimate is that about 80 percent of inventory shrinkage is due to theft and that some three-quarters of tat involves theft by store employees

**petit larceny:** the taking of property from a person, without that person's consent and with the intent to deprive the person permanently of the use of the property; distinguished from grand larceny by the value of the property stolen, with petit larceny involving a lower value; pronounced "petty" larceny

**psychosocial encapsulation:** a situation in which the offender can think of no way out of a dilemma other than crime

**robbery:** a form of theft in which goods or money is taken from a person against that person's will through the use of violence or fear

**shoplifting:** the stealing of goods from a retail store by stealth

**target hardening:** efforts to prevent burglary, such as better locks and windows

**telemarketing fraud:** involves the sale of worthless or greatly overpriced investment "opportunities" or other scams; it is carried out by contacting persons over the telephone and employing a scripted sales pitch to defraud them

**usury:** the lending of money at interest

**white-collar crime:** offenses committed by persons of high status in the course of their business, professional, or political lives, or any offense involving violations of laws such as the Sherman Act, which forbids conspiracies in restraint of trade, as well as statutes such as those that outlaw false advertising, embezzlement, and a very large number of laws that come under the general heading of fraud

## Key Criminologists

**John Braithwaite:** studied harms committed by industries, including a 1984 study of the pharmaceutical industry that documented in detail the "abominable harm" caused by illegal acts of drug companies

**Mary Owen Cameron:** undertook what stood for many years as the classical study of shoplifters, concluding that amateur shoplifters are not suffering from psychological disturbances but rather are respectable people who pilfer systematically

**Donald Cressey:** a renowned criminologist and student of Edwin Sutherland; he continued Sutherland's classic criminology text after Sutherland's death; he learned that embezzlers typically insisted that there were only borrowing the money

**Jack Katz:** analyzed shoplifting accounts obtained from primarily female criminology students at UCLA; he found that material needs were inadequate to account for their thefts and believed that, for the students, shoplifting was a tactic in a war against boredom rather than against poverty

**John and Lyn Lofland:** maintained that the decision to carry out most crimes involves a three-phase process, beginning with (1) a perceived threat (which often is to the offender's self-esteem), moving to (2) a state of "psychosocial encapsulation," and culminating in (3) the specific criminal act

**Henry Pontell:** studied white-collar crime; found that individuals involved in the S&L scandals engaged in "collective embezzlement," where they gained personally at the expense of the institutions

**E.A. Ross:** studied crimes of the well-placed, whom he labeled *criminals*

**Edwin H. Sutherland:** perhaps the best known criminologist of the twentieth century; he coined the term "white-collar crime"; he defined the behavior as involving illegal activities of persons of high status and argued that it could be explained by his theory of differential association

**Thorstein Veblen:** author of *Theory of the Leisure Class* (1912); studied crimes committed by persons in the higher echelons of society

Chapter 13

# Crimes without Victims
# and Victims without Crimes

## Summary

Victimless crimes involve outlawed behaviors that are conducted by consenting parties. Examples of victimless crimes include prostitution, illegal gambling, and illicit drug use. Status offenses prohibit certain behaviors for only specified groups of people, such as those below a given age. Truancy and running away from home are examples of behaviors that are forbidden only for juveniles.

Victimless crimes are the subject of much debate. Critics claim that such legislation impinges upon personal freedoms. They point out that victimless offenses are often based on moral or religious arguments rather than some harm that may result form the behavior. They suggest that decriminalizing victimless offenses could benefit society in many ways. The legalization of drugs, for example, would remove the necessity of addicts to steal to support their habits, prevent the drug trade from being controlled by organized crime, and make sterile needles available so that AIDS would not spread. Several victimless offenses have been decriminalized. Examples include abortion, gambling, and homosexual activity. It has been suggested that these behaviors were removed from criminal codes because powerful persons engaged in them. Supporters of these crimes argue that there is no such thing as a victimless crime. For example, prostitution spreads disease, causes family problems, and supports other forms of crimes.

## Physician-Assisted Suicide

Dr. Jack Kevorkian's participation in physician-assisted suicides brought the issue to the current level of debate. The question of whether one has a right to suicide assistance or whether this is criminal is currently in the hands of each state. The debate raises many ethical and practical issues. Currently, the only jurisdiction in the United States to allow physician-assisted suicide is the state of Oregon.

## Prostitution—Sex Work

Feminists disagree on the definition of prostitution. Liberal feminists view it as a sensible commercial enterprise. Radical feminists, on the other hand, see it as the sexual exploitation of female integrity due to the power of men over women. They point to pimps as an example of patriarchal control of prostitution. Prostitution is legal in England, although many of the activities peripheral to it, such as soliciting and loitering, remain criminalized. In the United States, prostitution is legal only in 14 of Nevada's 17 counties; it occurs, however, in only 11 counties, where there are 28 brothels. Studies have shown that prostitutes who work in areas where the activity is legal have a lower rate of AIDS.

Although female prostitution is by far the most prevalent form, men also engage in this activity. In the United States, men often seek to form liaisons with older men who will support them. Male prostitutes, like female prostitutes, are motivated by financial incentives. Today, prostitutes of both sexes often use the Internet to contact potential partners.

## Drug Offenses

Drug offenders now comprise about 70 percent of the inmate population in federal prisons. Those inmates serving time for drug-related offenses outnumber those serving time for manslaughter, sexual abuse, assault, and arson. The cost to taxpayers exceeds $20,000 annually per inmate.

The Harrison Act of 1914 first outlawed opiates in the United States. Following this legislation, opiate addiction became concentrated in the lower socioeconomic classes. In upholding the legality of civil commitment programs, the courts changed the definition of addiction from a crime to an illness in *Robinson v. California* (1962). However, the only changes resulting from this ruling were basically related to terminology rather than practice.

Criminologists studying drug usage have suggested that drugs are a reflection of other problems experienced by the user. They reject the idea that drug users need to be rehabilitated because this term implies that the addict previously had a good way of life. These researchers suggest that drug addicts be habilitated, or socialized into a productive and responsible lifestyle that was previously unknown to them.

The Marijuana Tax Act of 1937 effectively banned the possession and use of marijuana. There is some evidence that marijuana was outlawed based on racial and ethnic prejudice rather than a concern for public health. Research on the health risk of marijuana has produced uncertain and contradictory results, and legislation regarding it has been based on ideology. Too, there have been recent debates concerning the use of marijuana for certain medical purposes. Critics of legislation against marijuana claim that it generates hostility toward the police and the law by needlessly labeling those who use marijuana as criminals. They highlight the vast amounts of funds spent in trying to control marijuana usage and point out that, being illegal, the sale of marijuana is controlled by organized criminal forces that also engage in more dangerous crimes. Ronald Akers views the use of marijuana as a product of differential association. Both the frequency and the quantity of drugs consumed by an individual are correlated with the number of friends who are current users. Finn-Aage Esbensen and Delbert Elliott have found that marriage and having a child increase the likelihood that a person will stop using illegal drugs.

## Victims without Crimes

Unlike the United States and England, all continental European countries have laws requiring that people in a position to do so must give aid to others in distress if they can do so without risk to themselves. Failing to give aid can result in a criminal charge. Graham Hughes, a criminal law scholar, believes that in a civilized society, everyone has a duty to extend help to those in need.

The cigarette industry offers the best illustration of victims without crimes. The tobacco industry makes large profits and uses those profits to protect itself from regulation. Knowing that their product contains a highly addictive substance—nicotine—and knowing that cigarette smoking has been linked to higher cancer and death rates, the industry leaders still sought to develop a high-nicotine tobacco plant. Eventually, the government stepped in and negotiated settlements between the tobacco companies and those suffering from cigarette-related diseases and the families of those who had died from cigarette-related conditions.

## Key Terms

**cocaine:** derived from coca leaves; is a central nervous system stimulant that allows the user to exhibit bursts of energy and gregarious enthusiasm; it is expensive, creates a psychological and perhaps a physiological state of dependency, and after the brief initial flow of energy it send users into mild to severe depression

**crack cocaine:** a cocaine derivative that costs considerably less than regular cocaine and is smoked rather than snorted or sniffed, producing a rapid, potent high

**crank:** an amphetamine also known as "speed"

**crimes without victims:** offenses for which there is no complainant such as prostitution, gambling, or drug transactions

**ensoulment:** the moment when a fetus becomes an individual with a God-given right to life

**marijuana:** a drug that, although its possession is still criminalized, is not as strictly prohibited as in prior decades

**methamphetamine:** a central nervous system stimulant; also known as "crank," "speed," "go fast," and "meth"

**opiates:** highly addictive group of depressants that include heroin, morphine, laudanum, and codeine

**physician-assisted suicide:** controversial role of the physician to intentionally withhold treatments or to administer substances that will lead to death of the terminally ill patient earlier than would otherwise occur

**pimp:** man who takes most of a prostitute's earnings and, in return, offers her protection from customers and the police and real affection or a caricature of it

**prostitution:** the selling of sexual relations, which is illegal throughout the United States except for 15 of Nevada's 17 counties

**status offenses:** criminal offenses in which the stipulated behavior is outlawed only for specified categories of people, such as those below a certain age

**victims without crimes:** self-evident social harms that are not illegal under criminal law (e.g., cigarette smoking)

**witchcraft:** an early victimless crime for which thousands of women were executed in Europe and England

## Key Criminologists

**Ronald Akers:** views marijuana use as the outcome of a process of differential association

**Elliott Currie:** criminologist who noted the arguments put forth by those favoring the decriminalization of marijuana

**Nanette Davis:** feminist criminologist who notes that prostitution is a political issue

**Finn-Aage Esbensen:** criminologist who, with Delbert Elliott, found support for social learning variables affecting the initiation of drug use

**Erich Goode:** criminologist who maintains that the debate over the legal status of marijuana is fundamentally an ideological conflict incorporating very little factual information

**James Inciardi:** criminologist who studied persons engaging in the use of crack cocaine, noting that the drug use may be a reflection of the person's other problems rather than a cause of them; he further noted that "rehabilitation" implies returning to a former lifestyle and suggested that many crack cocaine users need "habilitation"

Edwin Schur: noted that some illegal behaviors lack a direct complaining victim

Franklin Zimring: criminologist who noted that some involved in the debate over pornography, though not favoring the practice, feel that it is protected by the First Amendment

# Chapter 14
# Current Issues in Criminology

## Summary

Crime has been seen as an important problem for several decades. Many Americans fear crime and are seeking answers to control crime. Some feel that gun control is the answer, while others feel that the situation is hopeless. There are several reasons why people may be preoccupied with crime. They may include such things as "fear fatigue," feelings of insecurity and unmanageability, media exploitation, migration of drug activity to previously insulated communities, difficult economic times with high rates of unemployment, and the ageing of the population. Threats of terrorism are also cause for alarm.

For these reasons, Americans seem to be moving in a more punitive direction. They are expressing a desire to become tougher on crime, and politicians are mimicking the attitude of the general population. The "three strikes, you're out" legislation is the epitome of the attitude of mainstream America and is a huge victory for "get tough" politicians. This legislation seems to have gathered the most hoopla, but it is, in fact, riddled with problems. In Seattle, where the "three-strikes" concept originated, police are experiencing serious side effects that may undermine any advantages that this legislation is supposed to provide. The Seattle police note that since the implementation of the three-strikes legislation, criminals are now more likely to resort to violence when cornered to avoid arrest. Once arrested, the offenders are less willing to plea bargain; their cases are often taken to full trial. This unduly burdens an already stressed court system, because the courts have neither the extra space nor the personnel to manage a heavy increase in caseloads.

Two other approaches that have been adopted in an attempt to respond to crime are Megan's law legislation and laws that penalize hate crimes.

## Terrorism

Terrorism involves an act of violence intended to create fear, targets active and innocent victims, and has a political purpose. Richard Rosenfeld believes that the study of terrorism should be a high priority. His belief is based on the theory that terrorism is different from the "common" forms of violence studied by most criminologists. Terrorists, who are convinced that their causes are righteous, often use the concept of divine approval as the basis for their attacks. They also consider their attacks to be symbolic acts. Some parts of the world view the U.S. as having launched a terrorist campaign in waging the war against Iraq.

Two important concepts should be considered when studying terrorism. One is that people's beliefs concerning terrorism are based on their values and on where they live. The other is that it is often difficult to determine who, exactly, is the terrorist or war criminal.

## State Crimes/Extraordinary Rendition

State crimes are those crimes committed by the ruling regime of a nation in order to achieve its own goals, either internal or geopolitical. The military, the national security agencies, and various policing forces typically carry out these crimes. One example thought by many to be a state crime is that of the Vietnam War. Many believe that this was an act of aggression against a country that was engaged in an internal conflict—a civil war. State crimes are very difficult to prosecute. It is often unclear who should be held accountable for state acts of aggression.

## War Crimes

War crimes are defined as violations of the treaties that designate the length a government, military, or civilian can go in pursuing victory. Genocide is the most prominent war crime. One problem is that it is the victor who decides who should be regarded as a war criminal. The case of Slobodan Milosevic is the most prominent case, to date, of an international war crime. The former Serbian president was the first former head of state to be tried before an international tribunal for war crimes. After a four-year trial, and just before an anticipated verdict, Milosevic died of a heart attack in a prison cell.

## Get-Tough Measures

For the past decade, public policy has gone in the direction of tougher penalties for criminal offenses. According to Zimring, a growing public distrust of government has heavily influenced this movement. The public does not believe that judges always act responsibly when dealing with criminals (that is, they do not impose appropriate sentences). Therefore, the public tends to favor mandatory sentences that eliminate the input from judges.

In 1993, the first "three strikes, you're out" measure became law. This law stated that an offender convicted of three violent crimes, three felonies, or two felonies with a later misdemeanor would automatically be sentenced to a lengthy prison term or to life imprisonment without the possibility of parole. Those opposed to three-strikes legislation point out that this law causes offenders to act more violently and makes those offenders who have been apprehended less likely to plea bargain. They also point to an overworked court system that is unable to keep up with the numerous offenders and the cost of keeping individuals incarcerated for long periods of time. Proponents contend that the measure effectively deters crime and is responsible for recent declines in crime rates.

Hate crimes have also been singled out as offenses needing special attention. A hate crime is a crime committed against a person, group of people, or their property because of their race, religion, sexual orientation, or ethnicity. Crimes against disabled people can also be included in this category. Those who favor hate crime legislation do so because they believe that some people in society require particular protection because there is already an element of animosity directed toward them. Others oppose hate crime legislation because punishing someone not on the basis of their acts but on the basis of their beliefs and motivations is wrong.

Another get-tough approach to crime has been the enactment of Megan's Law. This law, which was brought about by the brutal rape and murder of 7-year-old Megan Kanka, made it mandatory for all states to adopt some form of community notification program with regard to paroled sex offenders.

Although Megan's Law does provide an added sense of safety, keeping tabs on approximately 500,000 convicted U.S. sex offenders is too large an undertaking to be 100 percent effective. Opponents of the law sometimes point out that those convicted sex offenders who have completed their sentences do not deserve the "double jeopardy" involved in being forced to admit their status to a neighborhood. They cite instances of violence directed toward released sex offenders. Others believe that the safety of the neighborhood residents should be paramount and dismiss accusations of harassment.

## Through the Looking Glass

Predicting the future with regard to crime and the criminal justice system is difficult, if not impossible. However, it is likely that what has begun will likely continue in the same direction. Although the United States is one of a very few countries in the world that continues to use the death penalty, there is evidence that support for capital punishment is beginning to erode. The ageing of the population and the growing number of minorities will likely have an impact on crime in the future. It is also assumed that criminology will start to take a closer look at terrorist acts and homeland security issues.

Advancements in medical research and technology may bring about new medications that can break the physical dependence on illegal drugs. Perhaps, too, attitudes toward drug users will become more lenient, with less of an emphasis on prosecution and imprisonment. Research—particularly in the area of DNA—may bring about new ways to fight crime and solve older crimes.

## Key Terms

**assassination:** an ordered murder of a person who is believed to impede the goals of a group; it can be requested by organized groups such as the Mafia or even by governments; there is some speculation about whether the United Nations had unofficially supported an assassination of Saddam Hussein during the Persian Gulf crisis

**extraordinary rendition:** a procedure in which the government of the United States, or other countries, sends a foreign suspect to another country, under less humane conditions, for interrogation; torture is said to often occur; provides a context for consideration of national values and the manner in which such values should be taken into account in public policy

**hate crime:** a criminal offense committed against an individual, group of individuals, or their property because of their race, religion, sexual orientation, or ethnicity

**Megan's Law:** requires authorities to notify residents who life in the neighborhood where a person who committed a sex offense against a minor now resides after release from prison

**oath:** used in court to support the witnesses' claims that the information they are about to provide is true and accurate; due to the high degree of perjury, it has been proposed that the oath be abandoned

**political crimes:** crimes encompassing a wide spectrum of offenses; the exact definition is subject to debate, but can include crimes such as treason, assassinations, riots and violations by governments who spy on their own people, but the nature of the motivation is critical in the analyses of most criminologists

**state crimes:** those acts of persons holding office that are harmful to those they rule; though rarely prosecuted; they can be deemed to violate the law or offend standards of justice; the term often involves controversy, such as when it is applied to the waging of war in Vietnam

**terrorism:** acts that threaten the safety and security of a state; it can also refer to the method of combat in which random or symbolic victims are targets of violence

**three strikes, you're out:** anticrime measure borrowed from Washington state law and introduced by President Bill Clinton as part of the federal crime bill that would allow for the imposition of life sentences without parole for offenders who were convicted of committing a third crime of violence

**treason:** acts of betrayal against a state that threaten or undermine the authority of such state

**war crime:** violation of the treaties that designate how far a government, military, or civilian can go to pursue victory

## Key Criminologists

**George Cole:** criminal justice scholar who has attempted to trace developments in the field in the future; among other things, Cole believes that we will discover a chemical that possesses the ability to break the physical dependence on drugs

**Fyodor Dostoevsky:** Russian novelist who wrote *Crime and Punishment*

**Valerie Jenness:** participated in a study that found that hate crime laws serve to heighten prejudice, exacerbate social division, and add conflict to society

**Diana E.H. Russell:** criminologist very active in the current debate about pornography within the realm of criminal justice; members of the women's organizations believe pornography to convey misogynistic views that trigger violent responses toward women

**Kenneth D. Tunnell:** criminologist who notes that political crimes such as treason, insurrections, and espionage are often omitted from criminology texts

**Frank Zimring:** maintained that support for punitive measures for get-touch policies is heavily influenced by a growing public distrust of government